CONTEÚDO DIGITAL PARA ALUNOS

Cadastre-se e transforme seus estudos em uma experiência única de aprendizado:

1

Entre na página de cadastro:

https://sistemas.editoradobrasil.com.br/cadastro

2

Além dos seus dados pessoais e dos dados de sua escola, adicione ao cadastro o código do aluno, que garantirá a exclusividade do seu ingresso à plataforma.

4416363A5831117

3

Depois, acesse:

https://leb.editoradobrasil.com.br/

e navegue pelos conteúdos digitais de sua coleção **:D**

Lembre-se de que esse código, pessoal e intransferível, é valido por um ano. Guarde-o com cuidado, pois é a única maneira de você acessar os conteúdos da plataforma.

Editora do Brasil

BRINCANDO
COM INGLÊS

3
EDUCAÇÃO INFANTIL

RENATO MENDES CURTO JÚNIOR

Licenciado em Letras

Certificado de proficiência em Língua Inglesa pela Universidade de Michigan e TOEFL

Autor de livros de educação a distância

Professor de Língua Inglesa e Portuguesa na rede particular de ensino desde 1986

ANNA CAROLINA GUIMARÃES

Licenciada em Pedagogia

Especialista em Educação Infantil e Anos Iniciais

Especialista em Neuropsicopedagogia

Coordenadora pedagógica de Educação Básica

CIBELE MENDES

Mestre em Educação

Licenciada em Pedagogia

Certificado de proficiência em Língua Inglesa pela Fluency Academy

Coordenadora pedagógica de Educação Infantil aos Anos Finais do Ensino Fundamental

Editora do Brasil

Dados Internacionais de Catalogação na Publicação (CIP)
(Câmara Brasileira do Livro, SP, Brasil)

Curto Júnior, Renato Mendes
Brincando com inglês: educação infantil 3 / Renato Mendes Curto Júnior, Anna Carolina Guimarães, Cibele Mendes. – 1. ed. – São Paulo: Editora do Brasil, 2024. – (Brincando com)

ISBN 978-85-10-09506-8 (aluno)
ISBN 978-85-10-09502-0 (professor)

1. Língua inglesa (Educação infantil) I. Guimarães, Anna Carolina. II. Mendes, Cibele. III. Título. IV. Série.

24-193929 CDD-372.21

Índices para catálogo sistemático:

1. Língua inglesa : Educação infantil 372.21

Cibele Maria Dias - Bibliotecária - CRB 8/9427

1ª edição / 1ª impressão, 2024
Impresso na Hawaii Gráfica e Editora

Editora do Brasil

Avenida das Nações Unidas, 12901
Torre Oeste, 20º andar
São Paulo, SP – CEP: 04578-910
Fone: +55 11 3226-0211
www.editoradobrasil.com.br

Direção-geral: Paulo Serino de Souza

Diretoria editorial: Felipe Ramos Poletti
Gerência editorial de conteúdo didático: Erika Caldin
Gerência editorial de produção e design: Ulisses Pires
Supervisão de design: Aurélio Gadini Camilo
Supervisão de arte: Abdonildo José de Lima Santos
Supervisão de revisão: Elaine Cristina da Silva
Supervisão de iconografia: Léo Burgos
Supervisão de digital: Priscila Hernandez
Supervisão de controle e planejamento editorial: Roseli Said
Supervisão de direitos autorais: Luciana Sposito

Supervisão editorial: Carla Felix Lopes e Diego da Mata
Edição: Danuza D. Gonçalves, Graziele Arantes, Natália Feulo, Sheila Fabre
Assistência editorial: Igor Gonçalves, Julia do Nascimento e Pedro Andrade Bezerra
Revisão: 2014 Soluções Editoriais, Alexander Barutti, Andréia Andrade, Beatriz Dorini, Bianca Oliveira, Gabriel Ornelas, Giovana Sanches, Jonathan Busato, Júlia Castello, Maisa Akazawa, Mariana Paixão, Martin Gonçalves, Rita Costa, Rosani Andreani, Sandra Fernandes e Yasmin Fonseca
Pesquisa iconográfica: Maria Santos e Selma Nagano
Tratamento de imagens: Robson Mereu
Projeto gráfico: Siamo Studio
Capa: Caronte Design
Imagem de capa: Graziela Andrade
Edição de arte: Daniele Fátima Oliveira e Yara Penteado Espírito Santo Anderi
Ilustrações: Ideario Lab e Claudia Marianno
Editoração eletrônica: Estúdio AbAeterno
Licenciamentos de textos: Cinthya Utiyama, Ingrid Granzotto, Renata Garbellini e Solange Rodrigues
Controle e planejamento editorial: Ana Fernandes, Bianca Gomes, Juliana Gonçalves, Maria Trofino, Terezinha Oliveira e Valéria Alves

APRESENTAÇÃO

QUERIDO ALUNO,

ESTE É O **BRINCANDO COM INGLÊS** EM SUA MAIS NOVA VERSÃO, PARA QUE O APRENDIZADO DA LÍNGUA INGLESA SE TORNE AINDA MAIS DIVERTIDO!

VOCÊ ENCONTRARÁ ATIVIDADES ESTIMULANTES E VIVENCIARÁ SITUAÇÕES DO DIA A DIA, PARA ESCUTAR, FALAR E APRENDER INGLÊS DE MODO NATURAL.

CADA AULA SERÁ UMA NOVA EXPERIÊNCIA, E VOCÊ NÃO VAI QUERER PARAR DE APRENDER!

VAMOS COMEÇAR?

OS AUTORES

CONHEÇA SEU LIVRO

SEJA BEM-VINDO À NOVA EDIÇÃO DO
BRINCANDO COM INGLÊS!

LET'S START

LOCALIZADA NO INÍCIO DE CADA VOLUME, ESTA SEÇÃO APRESENTA ATIVIDADES LÚDICAS QUE POSSIBILITAM PREPARAR OS ALUNOS PARA OS NOVOS CONTEÚDOS RETOMANDO CONTEÚDOS JÁ VISTOS.

COMPREHENSION

AS ATIVIDADES DESTA SEÇÃO VISAM À COMPREENSÃO DO TEXTO APRESENTADO NA ABERTURA DE UNIDADE.

LET'S PLAY

A SEÇÃO PROPÕE ATIVIDADES LÚDICAS RELACIONADAS À TEMÁTICA DA UNIDADE, COMO JOGO DE ERROS, APLICAÇÃO DE ADESIVOS ETC.

STICKERS

ADESIVOS PARA OS ALUNOS COLAREM EM DETERMINADAS ATIVIDADES.

LET'S LISTEN

O ALUNO TERÁ A OPORTUNIDADE DE OUVIR ÁUDIOS COM DIÁLOGOS E CANÇÕES PARA SE HABITUAR COM A LÍNGUA INGLESA.

GOOD DEED

APRESENTA TEMÁTICAS DE CUNHO SOCIAL E ÉTICO RELACIONADAS AO ASSUNTO DE CADA UNIDADE. CONTEMPLA OS OBJETIVOS DE APRENDIZAGEM E DESENVOLVIMENTO PREVISTOS NA BNCC PARA A EDUCAÇÃO INFANTIL.

DIGITAL PLAY

A SEÇÃO PROPÕE ATIVIDADES QUE INCLUEM O USO DE TECNOLOGIA. DEVERÃO SER ORIENTADAS E ACOMPANHADAS PELO PROFESSOR.

ENGLISH AROUND THE WORLD

A SEÇÃO CONTEMPLA A DIMENSÃO INTERCULTURAL DA LÍNGUA INGLESA, DESTACANDO OS ASPECTOS CULTURAIS DE PAÍSES QUE UTILIZAM O INGLÊS COMO IDIOMA OFICIAL OU LÍNGUA FRANCA.

LET'S SING

A SEÇÃO PROPÕE CANÇÕES PARA O ALUNO OUVIR E CANTAR.

AFTER THIS UNIT I CAN

A SEÇÃO OFERECE AO ALUNO A OPORTUNIDADE DE FAZER UMA AUTOAVALIAÇÃO, ENTENDENDO OS PONTOS EM QUE ENCONTROU MAIS FACILIDADE OU MAIS DIFICULDADE.

VOCABULARY

VOCABULÁRIO BILÍNGUE COM OS VOCÁBULOS ESTUDADOS NOS TEXTOS APRESENTADOS.

REVIEW

AS ATIVIDADES DESTA SEÇÃO PROPÕEM A RETOMADA DO CONTEÚDO ESTUDADO.

PICTURE DICTIONARY

A SEÇÃO DISPONIBILIZA O VOCABULÁRIO ESTUDADO NO LIVRO E AS RESPECTIVAS IMAGENS.

CELEBRATIONS

ENCARTE QUE INCLUI ATIVIDADES RELACIONADAS A DATAS COMEMORATIVAS.

ÍCONES

DESENHAR

COLORIR

FALAR OU CONVERSAR

TRAÇAR OU ESCREVER

CANTAR

ADESIVO

DESTACAR

CIRCULAR

MARCAR

CONTAR

ESCUTAR

ENCONTRAR

COLAR

RECORTAR

LIGAR/ RELACIONAR

APONTAR

CONTENTS

LET'S START!........8

UNIT 1
SCHOOL FRIENDS........19

UNIT 2
FUN TIME........31

UNIT 3
ONLINE GAMES........43

UNIT 4
MY HEROES........53

UNIT 5
FAMILY VACATION........67

UNIT 6
HEALTHY FOOD........79

UNIT 7
A VISIT TO THE AQUARIUM...89

UNIT 8
TRASH? OH NO!........101

REVIEW........111

PICTURE DICTIONARY........119

INDEX OF SONGS........127

INDEX OF LISTENINGS........128

CELEBRATIONS........129

STICKERS........145

LET'S START!

1 MATCH THE CHILDREN TO THEIR PETS.

Ideario Lab

ORANGE

BROWN

GRAY

YELLOW

BLACK

GlobalP/iStockphoto.com

5 second Studio/Shutterstock.com

Boonchuay Promjiam/Shutterstock.com

ViachaslauKraskouski/iStockphoto.com

pritsana/Shutterstock.com

2 FIND **SIX** DIFFERENCES AND TRACE THE WORD.

Ideario Lab

macrojobs/
Shutterstock.com

I  PETS

3 LOOK AND NUMBER.

1 – KITCHEN
2 – LIVING ROOM
3 – BEDROOM
4 – BATHROOM
5 – LAUNDRY

Claudia Marianno

4 TAKE YOUR FRIENDS TO THE WATER PARK.
PASTE THE STICKERS.

Ilustrações: Ideario Lab

Ideario Lab

5 MATCH.

evgenyatamanenko/iStockphoto.com

GOOD AFTERNOON

Oksana Kuzmina/Shutterstock.com

GOOD MORNING

Anna Kraynova/Shutterstock.com

GOOD NIGHT

Ground Picture/Shutterstock.com
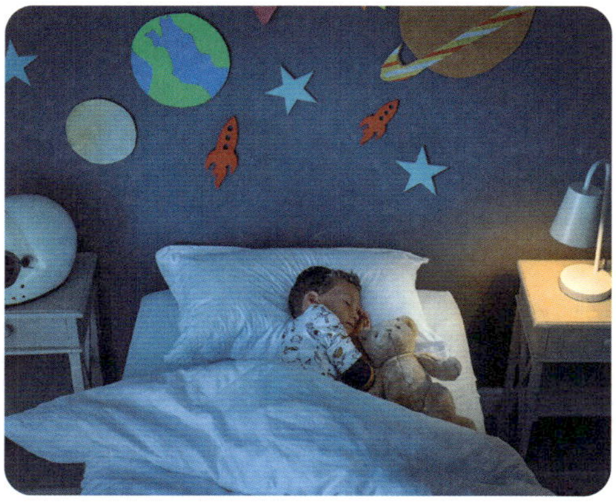

GOOD EVENING

6 TRACE THE WORDS.

Granate Art/Shutterstock.com

SCHOOL

moloko_vector/Shutterstock.com

STUDENT

Volha Hlinskaya/Shutterstock.com

TEACHER

7 LOOK AND TRACE THE NUMBERS.

3 THREE

6 SIX

8 EIGHT

4 FOUR

5 FIVE

1 ONE

2 TWO

10 TEN

9 NINE

7 SEVEN

Claudia Marianno

8 COUNT AND WRITE.

Ideario Lab

9 TRACE THE WORDS.

MOTHER

FATHER

DAUGHTER

SON

10 MATCH THE NAME WITH THE CORRECT FAMILY MEMBER.

Claudia Marianno

11 DRAW YOUR FAMILY.

12 LOOK AND TRACE.

rcherem/Shutterstock.com

HAPPY

SAD

13 HELP AVA FIND HER **RED** BACKPACK.

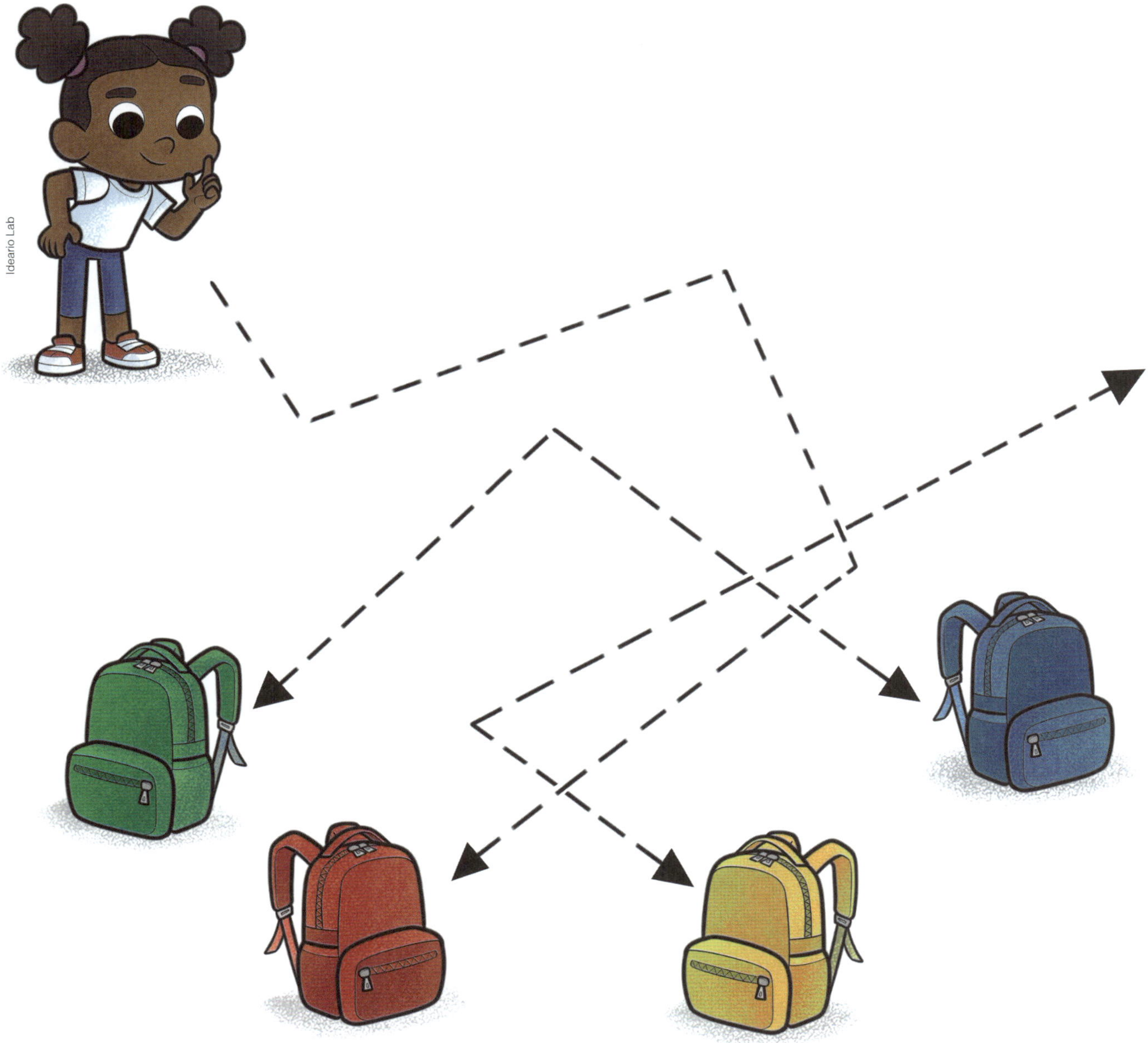

Ideario Lab

- HOW MANY BACKPACKS ARE THERE? WRITE.

FOUR

14 WHERE DO THE BOYS LIVE? FIND THE WAY.

yaruta/iStockphoto.com

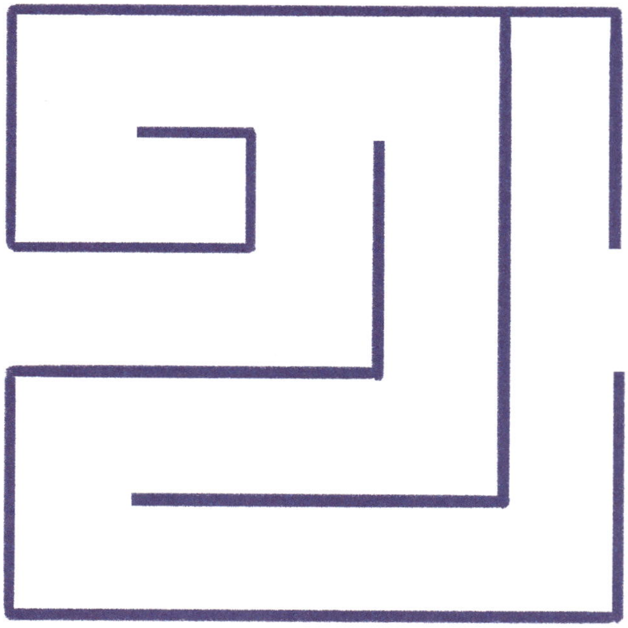

Claudia Marianno

ChameleonsEye/Shutterstock.com

15 CHECK THE TOYS YOU SEE IN THE PICTURE.

Claudia Marianno

- [ ] BALL
- [ ] BIKE
- [ ] DOLL
- [ ] SKATE
- [ ] TEDDY BEAR
- [ ] YO-YO

UNIT 1

SCHOOL FRIENDS

WHAT'S UP? MY NAME IS AVA. THESE ARE MY SCHOOL FRIENDS.
I AM TIM. I'M FIVE YEARS OLD.
NICE TO MEET YOU! MY NAME IS JAY.
HI, I'M MIA. I'M FIVE TOO.
HELLO! MY NAME IS ERIC. I'M SIX YEARS OLD.
HELLO! I'M SOPHIA. NICE TO MEET YOU!

Ideario Lab

VOCABULARY

I AM/I'M: EU SOU.

WHAT'S UP?: COMO VAI?/ COMO ESTÁ?

SCHOOL: ESCOLA.

I'M FIVE/SIX YEARS OLD: EU TENHO CINCO/SEIS ANOS.

HI: OI.

NICE TO MEET YOU!: PRAZER EM CONHECÊ-LO!

MY NAME IS...: MEU NOME É...

HELLO: OLÁ.

COMPREHENSION

1. WHERE ARE THE KIDS? CHECK.

icemanphotos/Shutterstock.com

hanohiki/Shutterstock.com

giedre vaitekune/Shutterstock.com

☐ ON THE BEACH. ☐ IN A CONDOMINIUM. ☐ AT SCHOOL.

2. WHO SPEAKS FIRST? CIRCLE.

Ideario Lab

MIA ERIC JAY TIM AVA SOPHIA

3. HOW MANY KIDS ARE THERE? CHECK.

☐ 5 (FIVE) ☐ 6 (SIX) ☐ 7 (SEVEN)

LET'S PLAY

1 COMPLETE WITH THE MISSING NUMBERS.

| 1 | 2 | 3 | 4 | 5 |

| 6 | 7 | 8 | 9 | 10 |

| 11 | 12 | 13 | 14 | 15 |

2 TRACE THE WORDS.

11 ELEVEN

12 TWELVE

13 THIRTEEN

14 FOURTEEN

15 FIFTEEN

LET'S LISTEN

1 LISTEN.

A

fuatprasetya/Shutterstock.com

APPLE

B

VectorsMarket/Shutterstock.com

BEE

C

fuatprasetya/Shutterstock.com

CAT

D

Tartila/Shutterstock.com

DOLPHIN

E

fuatprasetya/Shutterstock.com

ELEPHANT

F

fuatprasetya/Shutterstock.com

FISH

G

NatiArty/Shutterstock.com

GIRAFFE

H

fuatprasetya/Shutterstock.com

HOUSE

I

fuatprasetya/Shutterstock.com

ICE CREAM

J

Nsit/Shutterstock.com

JELLY

K

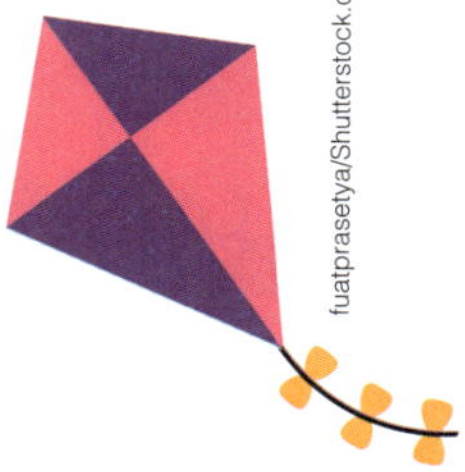

fuatprasetya/Shutterstock.com

KITE

L

fuatprasetya/Shutterstock.com

LADYBIRD

M

fuatprasetya/Shutterstock.com

MOUSE

N

fuatprasetya/Shutterstock.com

NEWT

O

fuatprasetya/Shutterstock.com

OCTOPUS

P

Tartila/Shutterstock.com

PIG

Q

Tartila/Shutterstock.com

QUEEN

R

NatiArty/Shutterstock.com

ROCKET

S

Antonov Maxim/Shutterstock.com

SNAKE

T

Jemastock/Shutterstock.com

TEDDY BEAR

U

fuatprasetya/Shutterstock.com

UMBRELLA

V

Svet_Zhdan/Shutterstock.com

VASE

W

fuatprasetya/Shutterstock.com

WHALE

X

fuatprasetya/Shutterstock.com

XYLOPHONE

Y

fuatprasetya/Shutterstock.com

YO-YO

Z

fuatprasetya/Shutterstock.com

ZEBRA

2 CIRCLE THE VOWELS.

LET'S PLAY

1 COLOR AND TRACE THE CONSONANTS.

AmazeinDesign/Shutterstock.com

BOAT

B

B B B B B B B B B B B B B

GlobalP/iStockphoto.com

CAT

C

C C C C C C C C C C C

LET'S LISTEN

1 LISTEN AND COLOR.

THIS IS MY FRIEND.
SCHOOL
THIS IS MY SCHOOL.
THIS IS MY STUDENT.
THIS IS MY TEACHER.
THIS IS MY SCHOOL MATERIAL.

Ideario Lab

LET'S PLAY

1 PASTE THE STICKERS. THEN MATCH THEM TO THE CORRECT NAMES.

SHARPENER

ERASER

RULER

Claudia Marianno

PENCIL

BOOK

PENCIL CASE

LET'S SING!

HELLO, HELLO, HELLO

HELLO, HELLO, HELLO
MY NAME IS MIA
I'M FIVE YEARS OLD
NICE TO MEET YOU!

HI, HI, HI
MY NAME IS ERIC
I'M SIX YEARS OLD
NICE TO MEET YOU!

HELLO, HELLO, HELLO
MY NAME IS TIM
I'M FIVE YEARS OLD
NICE TO MEET YOU!

HI, HI, HI
MY NAME IS AVA
I'M SIX YEARS OLD

WHAT'S YOUR NAME?
WHAT'S YOUR NAME?
WHAT'S YOUR NAME?

SPECIALLY WRITTEN FOR THIS BOOK.

Ideario Lab

VOCABULARY

HELLO: OLÁ.

MY NAME IS: MEU NOME É.

NICE TO MEET YOU!: PRAZER EM CONHECÊ-LO!

HI: OI.

I'M FIVE/SIX YEARS OLD: EU TENHO 5/6 ANOS.

WHAT'S YOUR NAME?: QUAL É O SEU NOME?

DIGITAL PLAY

LET'S PLAY WITH THE LETTERS!

JuShoot/iStockphoto.com

WHAT IS YOUR NAME?

ENGLISH AROUND THE WORLD

GREETINGS AROUND THE WORLD

- HOW DO YOU GREET YOUR FRIENDS?

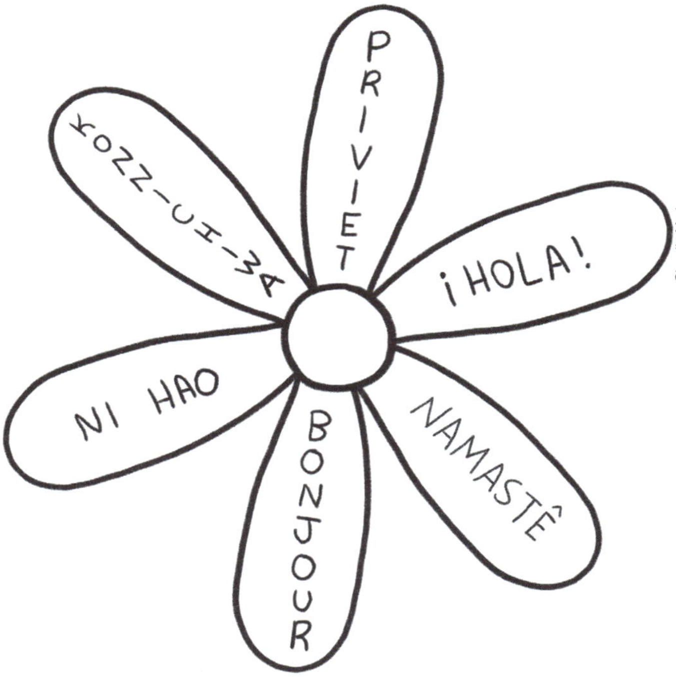

Claudia Marianno

GOOD DEED

BE HAPPY! BE A REAL FRIEND!

I RESPECT MY FRIENDS AND THE SCHOOL STAFF.

Sunny studio/Shutterstock.com

- COLOR THE WORDS.

BE A REAL
FRIEND!

LET'S PLAY

1 WHAT IS THE STICKER? PASTE EACH ONE ACCORDING TO THE CAPTION.

HAPPY. ANGRY. CREATIVE.

AFTER THIS UNIT I CAN

USE DIFFERENT GREETINGS.			
TALK ABOUT AGE.			
IDENTIFY VOWELS AND CONSONANTS **B** AND **C**.			
LEARN THE ALPHABET.			
USE NUMBERS 1-15.			
VALUE THE RESPECT AMONG FRIENDS.			

UNIT 2

FUN TIME

CHILDREN, TIME TO PLAY!
I CAN JUMP ROPE!
I CAN RUN!
I CAN PLAY!
I CAN DRAW!
Ideario Lab

VOCABULARY

TIME TO PLAY: HORA DE BRINCAR.

I CAN: EU CONSIGO.

JUMP ROPE: PULAR CORDA.

RUN: CORRER.

PLAY: JOGAR.

DRAW: DESENHAR.

COMPREHENSION

1 COLOR AND MATCH.

Ideario Lab

Pixel-Shot/Shutterstock.com

YuliDor/Shutterstock.com

Editable line icons/ Shutterstock.com

2 WHAT ARE THE CHILDREN DOING?

Olga1818/Shutterstock.com

☐ THEY ARE STUDYING. ☐ THEY ARE PLAYING.

LET'S

LISTEN

1 PASTE THE STICKER. THEN, MATCH.

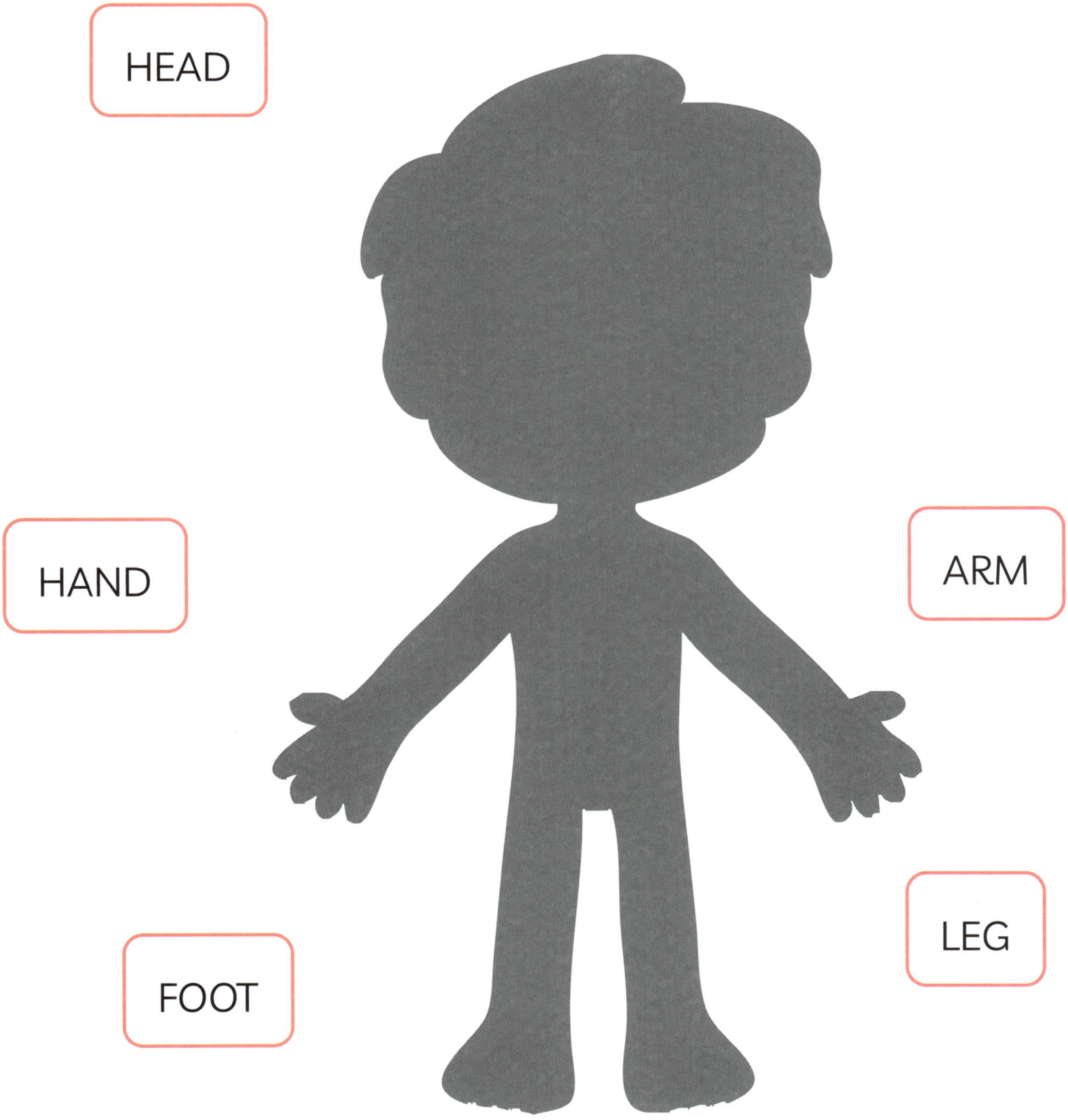

LET'S PLAY

1 TRACE THE LINES.

Onica Alexandru Sergiu/Shutterstock.com

DRAW

yusufdemirci/Shutterstock.com

JUMP

Iconic Bestiary/Shutterstock.com

RUN

DIGITAL PLAY

SCHOOL RUN

- LISTEN TO THE TEACHER'S INSTRUCTIONS AND FOLLOW THEM.

klyaksun/Shutterstock.com

2 FIND OUT AND MARK **SEVEN** DIFFERENCES.

GOOD DEED

LET'S HAVE FUN WITH EDUCATION AND RESPECT

Elena Brovko/iStockphoto.com

GOLDEN RULES

- WE SAY PLEASE AND THANK YOU.
- WE LISTEN TO THE TEACHER.
- WE FOLLOW DIRECTIONS.
- WE RESPECT EACH OTHER.

- LOOK AT THE PICTURE.

Lisitsa/iStockphoto.com

- DO YOU GET ALONG WITH YOUR CLASSMATES?

I CAN DO MANY THINGS!

LET'S SING!

Ideario Lab

IT'S A BIRTHDAY! CLAP YOUR HANDS!
ARE YOU THINKING? TOUCH YOUR HEAD!
I SAW A COCKROACH!
TAP YOUR FEET!

WILL IT RAIN? TURN AROUND!
TIRED OF WALKING? RIDE A BIKE!
I SAW A HUGE SNAKE!
JUMP HIGH!

I CAN HOP LIKE A BUNNY
I CAN JUMP LIKE A FROG
I CAN DO MANY THINGS WITH MY BODY
I CAN SWIM LIKE A DOLPHIN
I CAN RUN LIKE A DOG
I CAN DO MANY THINGS WITH MY BODY

WRITTEN SPECIALLY FOR THIS BOOK.

VOCABULARY

CLAP YOUR HANDS: BATA PALMAS.

TOUCH YOUR HEAD: TOQUE SUA CABEÇA.

TAP YOUR FEET: BATA OS PÉS.

TURN AROUND: VIRE-SE.

JUMP HIGH: PULE ALTO.

LET'S PLAY

1 MATCH.

Evgeny Atamanenko/Shutterstock.com

anatoliy_gleb/Shutterstock.com

Maria Symchych/Shutterstock.com

Gorloff-KV/Shutterstock.com

Ground Picture/Shutterstock.com

RIDE A BIKE

CLAP HANDS

STOMP FEET

TOUCH HEAD

JUMP

2 LOOK AT THE PICTURES. CHECK THE ONES THAT SHOW GOOD ACTIONS.

NotionPic/Shutterstock.com

Aleutie/iStockphoto.com

brgfx/Shutterstock.com

NotionPic/Shutterstock.com

pijama61/iStockphoto.com

Bakhauaddin-bek Sopybekov/iStockphoto.com

GAMES AROUND THE WORLD

1 CHILDREN ALL OVER THE WORLD ENJOY PLAYING. TAKE A LOOK!

A) 

exxorian/iStockphoto.com

HIDE-AND-SEEK.

C) 

blueringmedia/iStockphoto.com

HOPSCOTCH.

B) 

virtute/iStockphoto.com

TAG.

D) 

BlueRingMedia/Shutterstock.com

MUSICAL CHAIRS.

2 WHAT IS YOUR FAVORITE GAME?

LET'S PLAY

1 COLOR.

A)

Lunnaya/Shutterstock.com

B)

natasha-tpr/iStockphoto.com

2 LET'S HAVE FUN THE MAORI WAY. FOLLOW THE TEACHER'S INSTRUCTIONS.

Album/Easypix Brasil

AFTER THIS UNIT

I CAN

LEARN THE VOCABULARY OF PHYSICAL ABILITIES.			
REVIEW THE NAMES OF THE BODY PARTS.			
IDENTIFY VERBS RELATED TO MOVEMENTS.			
LEARN THE NAMES OF GAMES IN ENGLISH.			

UNIT 3

ONLINE GAMES

GOOD AFTERNOON, TEAM. WELCOME TO OUR VIDEO GAME COMPETITION! ARE YOU READY TO START THE GAME?
COOL! WE WANT TO BE THE WINNERS!
GAME
THIS GYMNASIUM IS AWESOME!
GREAT! I LOVE VIDEO GAMES! THEY MAKE US MORE INTELLIGENT!

Ideário Lab

VOCABULARY

GOOD AFTERNOON: BOA TARDE.

WELCOME: BEM-VINDOS.

READY: PRONTOS.

START: COMEÇAR.

GREAT: SENSACIONAL.

COOL: LEGAL.

WANT (TO WANT): QUEREMOS (QUERER).

WINNERS: VENCEDORES(AS).

AWESOME: INCRÍVEL.

COMPREHENSION

1 WHERE ARE THE CHILDREN GOING TO PLAY? CHECK.

the8monkey/Shutterstock.com

☐ AT A THEATER.

Tartila/Shutterstock.com

☐ IN A CLASSROOM.

Seahorse Vector/Shutterstock.com

☐ IN A GYMNASIUM.

2 WHO LOVES ONLINE GAMES?

☐ JAY AND ERIC.

☐ MIA.

☐ TIM AND AVA.

LET'S LISTEN

1 CIRCLE THE GAME WORDS YOU KNOW.

LET'S PLAY

1 PASTE THE STICKERS.

kiyaksun/Shutterstock.com

GAME LEVELS.

PixelChoice/Shutterstock.com

START NEW GAME.

Unitone Vector/Shutterstock.com

WINNER / LOSER

robuart/Shutterstock.com

GAME OVER.

2 TRACE THE NUMBERS AND COUNT.

Tatiana Arestova/Shutterstock.com

ONE TWO THREE

FOUR FIVE SIX SEVEN

EIGHT NINE TEN ELEVEN

TWELVE THIRTEEN FOURTEEN FIFTEEN

LET'S LISTEN

1 LISTEN TO THE NUMBERS.

ONE
1

TWO
2

THREE
3

FOUR
4

FIVE
5

SIX
6

SEVEN
7

EIGHT
8

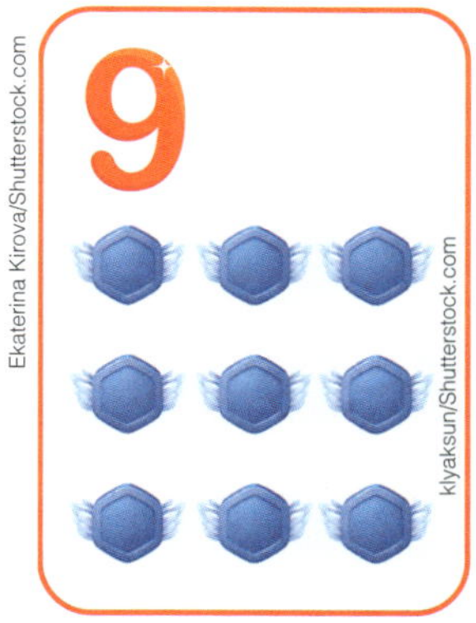

NINE
9

TEN
10

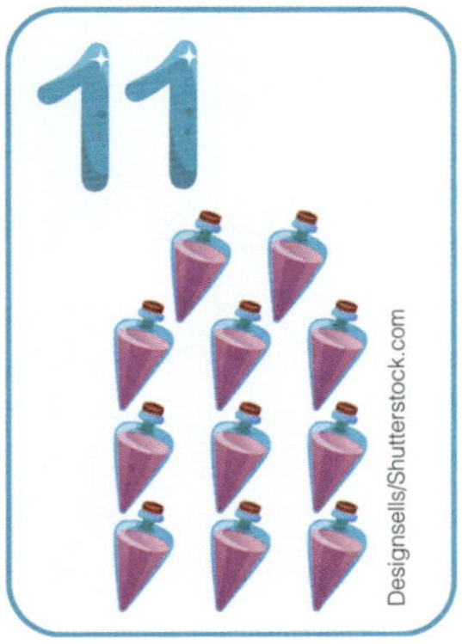

ELEVEN
11

TWELVE
12

THIRTEEN
13

FOURTEEN
14

FIFTEEN
15

GOOD DEED

VIDEO GAMES

DID YOU KNOW THAT PLAYING VIDEO GAMES CAN IMPROVE YOUR MEMORY AND HELP YOU MAKE NEW FRIENDS?

- PLAY A GAME AND CHECK YOUR MEMORY!

Miljan Zivkovic/Shutterstock.com

DIGITAL PLAY

CAN YOU CHANGE LEVELS?

- FIND AND CIRCLE THE HIGHEST LEVEL OF THE GAME.

klyaksun/Shutterstock.com

LET'S SING!

I LIKE VIDEO GAMES

ARE YOU PLUGGED IN? (YEAH!)
ALRIGHT, READY?
ONE, TWO, A-ONE, TWO, THREE!

I PLAY VIDEO GAMES
I LIKE TO PLAY AND HAVE FUN
I LIKE, I LIKE, I LIKE

ARE YOU PLUGGED IN? (YEAH!)
ALRIGHT, READY?
ONE, TWO, A-ONE, TWO, THREE!
I PLAY VIDEO GAMES
I HAVE FRIENDS
I WIN, I WIN, I WIN!

ARE YOU PLUGGED IN? (YEAH!)
ALRIGHT, READY?
ONE, TWO, A-ONE, TWO, THREE!

SPECIALLY WRITTEN FOR THIS BOOK.

Ideario Lab

VOCABULARY

PLUGGED IN: CONECTADO.
ALRIGHT: TUDO CERTO.
READY: PRONTO.
FRIENDS: AMIGOS.

ENGLISH AROUND THE WORLD

- SOME GAMES ARE PLAYED ALL OVER THE WORLD. CHECK THE CHARACTERS YOU KNOW.

Muza DS/Shutterstock.com

☐

alek7y/Shutterstock.com

☐

AleTorres/Shutterstock.com

☐

AFTER THIS UNIT I CAN

USE VIDEO GAME WORDS.

USE NUMBERS FROM 1 TO 15.

IDENTIFY THE GAME CHARACTERS I KNOW.

UNIT 4

MY HEROES

I AM CAPTAIN AMERICA!
I'M PRINCESS ARIEL.
WOW! I AM WONDER WOMAN.
LOOK AT YOU! YOU LOOK INCREDIBLE!
I'M SPIDER-MAN, MY FAVORITE HERO.
WHO ARE YOU, JAY?
I AM SUPERMAN, AVA.

Ideario Lab

VOCABULARY

LOOK AT YOU: OLHEM PARA VOCÊS.

INCREDIBLE: INCRÍVEL.

WHO ARE YOU?: QUEM É VOCÊ?

WONDER WOMAN: MULHER-MARAVILHA.

SPIDER-MAN: HOMEM-ARANHA.

FAVORITE: FAVORITO.

HERO: HERÓI.

I AM/I'M: EU SOU.

PRINCESS: PRINCESA.

COMPREHENSION

1 WHAT IS JAY WEARING?

Alex Tsuper/Shutterstock.com

2 COLOR THE BOYS' COSTUMES.

Claudia Marianno

3 WHAT IS AVA WEARING? CHECK.

Eugenia Cherubini/Shutterstock.com

animeofficial/Shutterstock.com

colorfulpaint/Shutterstock.com

4 COLOR THE GIRLS' COSTUMES.

Iryna Boiko/Shutterstock.com

Claudia Marianno

AnnaGarmatiy/iStockphoto.com

LET'S LISTEN

1 LISTEN.

fizkes/Shutterstock.com

I AM A HEROIN.
I'M SAVING LIVES.

I AM A HERO.
I'M MAINTAINING
SAFETY AND ORDER.

Fractal Pictures/Shutterstock.com

hedgehog94/Shutterstock.com

I AM A HEROIN.
I'M TAKING CARE
OF ANIMALS.

I AM A HEROIN. I'M
TEACHING YOU!

Robert Kneschke/Shutterstock.com

LET'S PLAY

1 COLOR.

SHE IS A HEROIN.
SHE SAVES LIVES.

pijama61/iStockphoto.com

2 MATCH THE REAL-LIFE HEROES TO THEIR PROFESSIONS.

passengerz/Shutterstock.com

DRIVER.

Ivan Mordvinkin/iStockphoto.com

FARMER.

Zentangle/Shutterstock.com

GARBAGE MAN.

AriSys/Shutterstock.com

POLICE OFFICER.

AGRICULTURE

CONSTRUCTION

POLICE

RECYCLING BINS

LET'S

LISTEN

1 LISTEN TO THE WORDS.

omravestudio/ Shutterstock.com

HOUSE.

yusufdemirci/Shutterstock.com

HAPPY.

grmarc/Shutterstock.com

HEART.

Magyro/Shutterstock.com

HAT.

2 CHECK THE WORDS THAT START WITH THE LETTER **H**.

Macrovector/Shutterstock.com

HERO

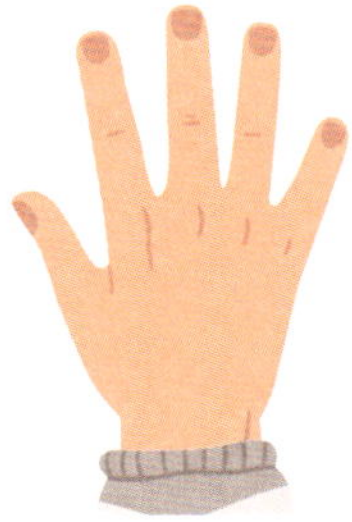
GoodStudio/Shutterstock.com

HAND

Kukulevskii/Shutterstock.com

PENCIL

Tenstudio/Shutterstock.com

HEAD

DIGITAL PLAY

OUR HEROES

1 WHO ARE YOUR HEROES?

MarkM73/iStockphoto.com

2 TRACE THE WORD.

HEROES

ENGLISH AROUND THE WORLD

- CIRCLE THE **BRAZILIAN** FLAG.

Piin_Petunyia/iStockphoto.com

Daria Ahafonova/Shutterstock.com

LightFieldStudios/iStockphoto.com

LET'S PLAY

1. LOOK AT THE IMAGES AND COMPLETE THE CROSSWORD PUZZLE.

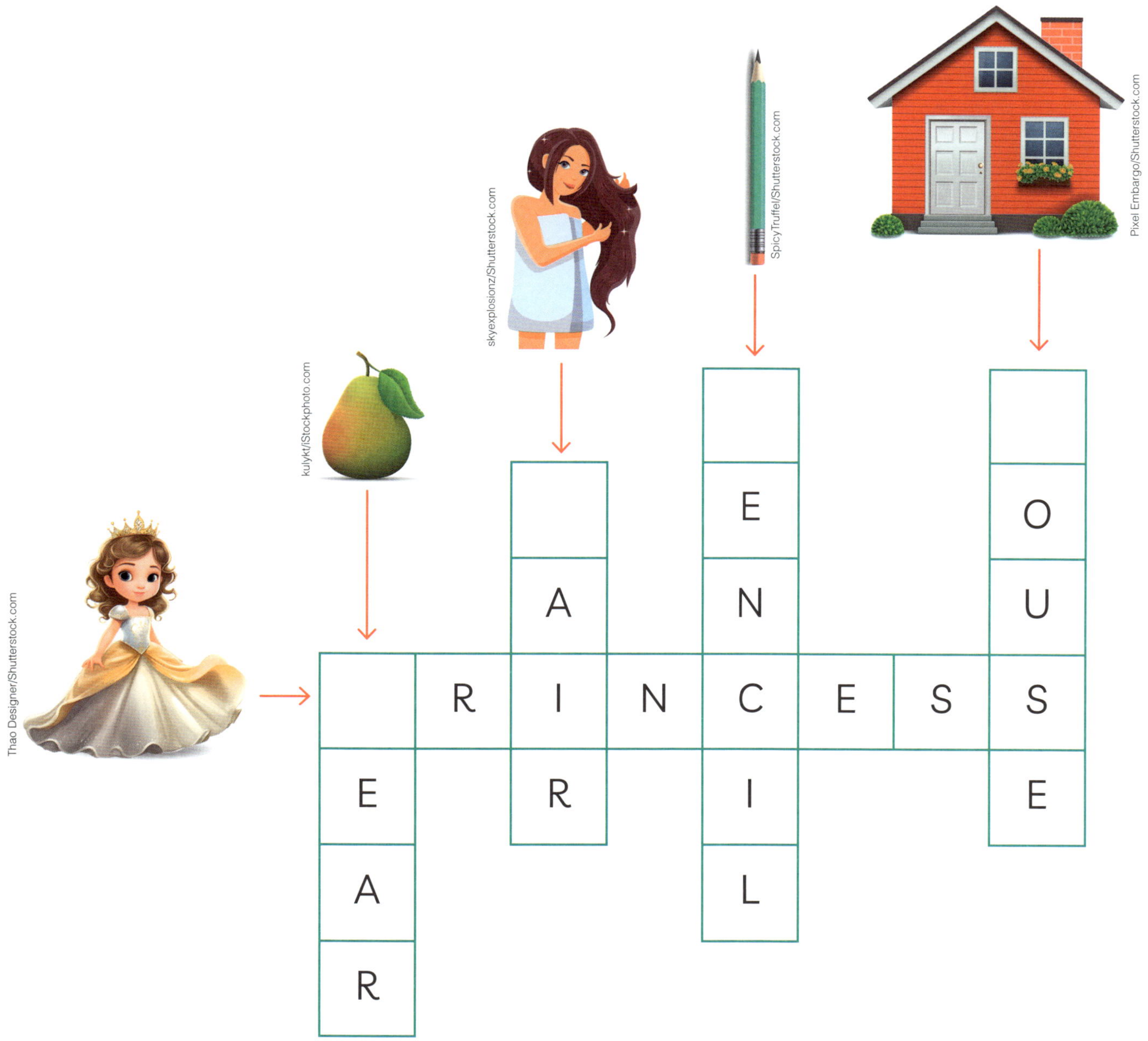

LET'S SING!

DO YOU WANT TO BE A HERO?

YES, YES, YES
NO, NO, NO
DO YOU WANT TO BE A HERO? YES.
DO YOU WISH TO BE EVIL? NO.

NOW BECOME SUPERMAN,
BATMAN, OR SPIDER-MAN
WHO HAS THE SKILL
WHO HAS THE SKILL
ALWAYS SENDS EVIL AWAY
AND THE BAD GUY ALWAYS GETS IT
AND THE BAD GUY ALWAYS GETS IT

VOCABULARY

WANT (TO WANT): QUER (QUERER).

HERO: HERÓI.

WISH (TO WISH): DESEJA (DESEJAR).

EVIL: MAL.

SKILL: HABILIDADE.

Ilustrações: Ideario Lab

YES, YES, YES
NO, NO, NO
DO YOU WANT TO BE A HERO? YES.
DO YOU WISH TO BE EVIL? NO.

NOW BECOME A PRINCESS OR A
WONDER WOMAN
WHO ALWAYS SHINES
WHO ALWAYS SHINES
ENCHANTS, AND BRINGS JOY
AND ALWAYS BRAVELY
AND ALWAYS BRAVELY

YES, YES, YES
YES, YES, YES
DO YOU WANT TO BE A HERO? YES.
A REAL HERO!

SPECIALLY WRITTEN
FOR THIS BOOK.

VOCABULARY

ALWAYS: SEMPRE.
BRINGS JOY: TRAZ ALEGRIA.
BRAVELY: COM VALENTIA.

GOOD DEED

BE A REAL-LIFE HERO!

- WOULD YOU LIKE TO BE A REAL-LIFE HERO? TALK ABOUT IT.

standret/iStockphoto.com

LET'S PLAY

1. COUNT AND TRACE THE NUMBERS.

TEN ELEVEN TWELVE THIRTEEN FOURTEEN FIFTEEN

aekikuis/Shutterstock.com

2 MATCH.

Germesia/Shutterstock.com

HAT

GreenSkyStudio/Shutterstock.com

HOUSE

Kashtanowww/Shutterstock.com

PRINCESS

Tartila/Shutterstock.com

HERO

Liana2012/iStockphoto.com

PENCIL

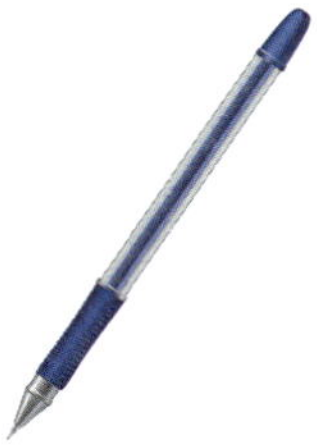

Duda Vasilii/Shutterstock.com

PEN

3 WHO ARE THE HEROES? PASTE THE STICKERS.

WONDER WOMAN.

SUPERMAN.

CAPTAIN AMERICA.

BATMAN.

AFTER THIS UNIT

I CAN

IDENTIFY HEROS, HEROINES, PRINCE AND PRINCESS.

RECOGNIZE REAL-LIFE HEROES.

IDENTIFY WORDS THAT BEGIN WITH THE CONSONANTS **H** AND **P**.

UNDERSTAND THE IMPORTANCE OF HELPING THE WORLD BE A BETTER PLACE.

UNIT 5

FAMILY VACATION

HI, CHILDREN! DRAW A PICTURE OF YOUR FAMILY VACATION.
WHERE DID YOU GO ON YOUR VACATION?
MY FAMILY AND I WENT TO THE COUNTRYSIDE.
I WENT TO THE BEACH WITH MY FAMILY. AND YOU?
WOW! YOU WENT THERE BY TRAIN!

Ideario Lab

VOCABULARY

FAMILY: FAMÍLIA.
VACATION: FÉRIAS.
WHERE: ONDE.
GO: IR.
BEACH: PRAIA.
AND YOU?: E VOCÊ?
COUNTRYSIDE: CAMPO.
BY TRAIN: DE TREM.

COMPREHENSION

1 WHERE DID AVA GO ON HER VACATION? CHECK.

Sofia Kalach/iStockphoto.com

☐ TO THE BEACH.

denis_pc/iStockphoto.com

☐ TO THE COUNTRYSIDE.

Norbert9/Shutterstock.com

☐ TO A BIG CITY.

2 WHAT MEANS OF TRANSPORTATION DID JAY USE ON HIS VACATION? CHECK AND COLOR.

A)

fuatprasetya/Shutterstock.com

☐

C)

fuatprasetya/Shutterstock.com

☐

B)

fuatprasetya/Shutterstock.com

☐

D)

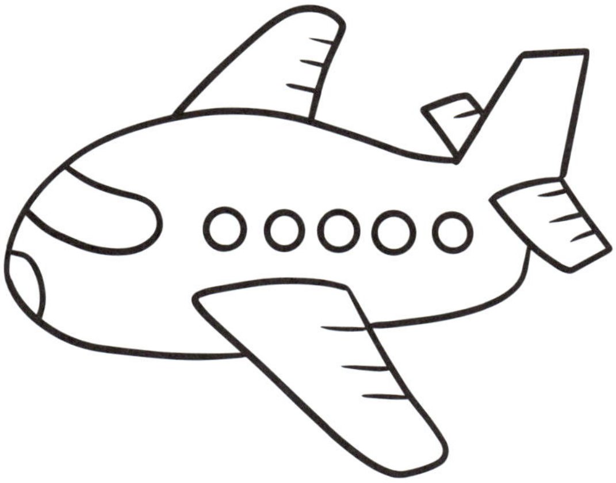

NatiArty/Shutterstock.com

☐

3 TRACE THE WORD.

TRAIN

LET'S LISTEN

1 LISTEN AND MATCH.

Ideario Lab

Monory/Shutterstock.com

BY AIRPLANE.

virtute/iStockphoto.com

BY TRAIN.

robuart/Shutterstock.com

BY BUS.

Igogosha/Shutterstock.com

BY CAR.

2 LOOK AND DRAW.

AIRPLANE.	BUS.	CAR.

GOOD DEED

POSITIVE ATTITUDES WHEN VISITING A PLACE

- COMPARE AND CHECK THE POSITIVE ATTITUDES.

A)

☐ 

Tenstudio/Shutterstock.com

☐ 

Moriz/Shutterstock.com

B)

☐ 

Wat cartoon/Shutterstock.com

☐ 

CoolFinger/Shutterstock.com

C)

☐ 

NotionPic/Shutterstock.com

☐ 

Tenstudio/Shutterstock.com

D)

☐ 

Colorfuel Studio/iStockphoto.com

☐ 

Colorfuel Studio/Shutterstock.com

LET'S PLAY

1 WHO IS PLAYING AT THE BEACH? PASTE THE STICKER AND FIND OUT!

2 WHERE IS THE GIRL? TRACE THE WORD.

BEACH

LET'S LISTEN

1 LISTEN AND CIRCLE.

A) THE RED CAR.

Dimitris Leonidas/Shutterstock.com

B) THE GREEN TRAIN.

White Space Illustrations/Shutterstock.com

C) THE BLUE BUS.

nitinut380/Shutterstock.com

D) THE YELLOW AIRPLANE.

MIKHAIL GRACHIKOV/Shutterstock.com

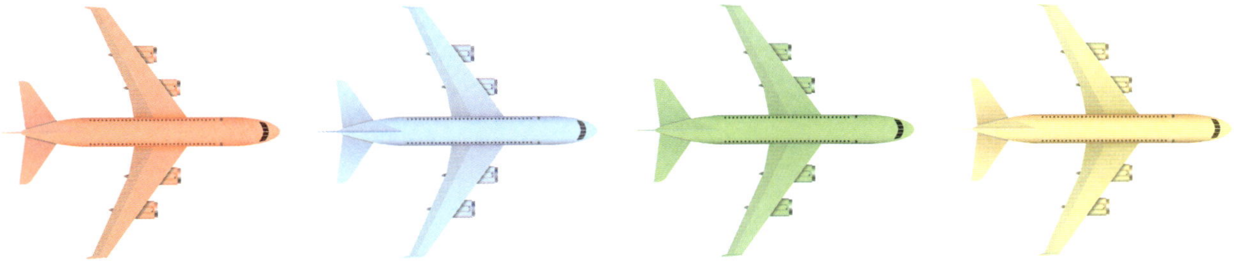

LET'S SING!

FAMILY VACATIONS

WE LOVE FAMILY VACATIONS,
IN THE COUNTRYSIDE AND AT THE BEACH.
UNDER THE SUN AND SAND ON OUR FEET.

WE WOKE UP EARLY, THE SUN WAS SHINING,
IN THE COUNTRYSIDE, IN THE FOREST, WE BEGAN TO EXPLORE,
TALL TREES AND BIRDS SINGING.

WE LOVE FAMILY VACATIONS,
IN THE COUNTRYSIDE AND AT THE BEACH.
UNDER THE SUN AND SAND ON OUR FEET.

Claudia Marianno

VOCABULARY

WE LOVE: NÓS AMAMOS.
FAMILY VACATIONS: FÉRIAS EM FAMÍLIA.
IN THE COUNTRYSIDE: NO CAMPO.
BEACH: PRAIA.
SUN: SOL.
SAND: AREIA.
FEET: PÉS.
WOKE UP: ACORDARMOS.
SHINING: BRILHANDO.
IN THE FOREST: NA FLORESTA.
BEGAN TO EXPLORE: COMEÇAMOS A EXPLORAR.
TALL TREES: ÁRVORES ALTAS.
BIRDS SINGING: PÁSSAROS CANTANDO.

AFTER A WHILE WE LEFT FOR THE SEA,
WITH THE GENTLE WAVES, IT'S TIME TO PLAY,
BUILD CASTLES IN THE SAND, DIVE IN THE SEA.

WE LOVE FAMILY VACATIONS,
IN THE COUNTRYSIDE AND AT THE BEACH.
UNDER THE SUN AND SAND ON OUR FEET.

WRITTEN FOR THIS BOOK.

VOCABULARY

AFTER A WHILE: DEPOIS DE UM TEMPO.

WE LEFT FOR THE SEA: FOMOS PARA O MAR.

BUILD CASTLES IN THE SAND: CONSTRUIR CASTELOS NA AREIA.

DIVE IN THE SEA: MERGULHAR NO MAR.

ENGLISH AROUND THE WORLD

TREASURE HUNT AROUND THE WORLD

LOOK AT THE TREASURES THAT REPRESENT THE CULTURAL SYMBOLS OF SOME ENGLISH-SPEAKING COUNTRIES.

ENGLAND	 bortonia/iStockphoto.com	 Robert Fruehauf/iStockphoto.com BIG BEN.
AUSTRALIA	 Kamlesh Suthar/iStockphoto.com	 GlobalP/iStockphoto.com KANGAROO.
THE UNITED STATES	 DrewTraveler/iStockphoto.com	 Freder/iStockphoto.com STATUE OF LIBERTY.
CANADA	 Lingkon Serao/iStockphoto.com	Valentina Razumova/ Shutterstock.com  MAPLE LEAF.

- CIRCLE THE CULTURAL SYMBOL YOU LIKED.

DIGITAL PLAY

TRAVELING WITHOUT LEAVING HOME

1 WHICH PLACE WOULD YOU LIKE TO VISIT?

A) MUSEUM OF NATURAL SCIENCES, IN THE USA.

zimmytws/Shutterstock.com

B) MUSEUM OF ART HISTORY, IN AUSTRIA.

Tupungato/Shutterstock.com

C) ACROPOLIS MUSEUM, IN GREECE.

saiko3p/Shutterstock.com

2 HOW ABOUT VISITING ONE OF THESE PLACES?

LET'S PLAY

1 WHERE IS THE MONSTER FAMILY?

Landmark Media/Alamy/Fotoarena

- [ ] IN THE COUNTRYSIDE.
- [ ] AT THE BEACH.

AFTER THIS UNIT I CAN

IDENTIFY VACATION PLACES.

RECOGNIZE MEANS OF TRANSPORTATION.

GET TO KNOW SOME CULTURAL SYMBOLS.

UNIT 6 HEALTHY FOOD

GOOD AFTERNOON. WHAT WOULD YOU LIKE TO EAT?
WOW! I LOVE THIS KIND OF FOOD! THEY'RE DELICIOUS AND HEALTHY.
Ideario Lab

VOCABULARY

GOOD AFTERNOON: BOA TARDE.

WOULD YOU LIKE: VOCÊ GOSTARIA.

EAT: COMER.

LOVE: AMO (AMAR).

KIND: TIPO.

FOOD: COMIDA.

HEALTHY: SAUDÁVEIS.

COMPREHENSION

1 WHERE ARE THEY? CHECK.

Evellean/Shutterstock.com

☐ AT SCHOOL.

inspiring.team/Shutterstock.com

☐ AT THE MALL.

Gvardgraph/Shutterstock.com

☐ IN A RESTAURANT.

2 WHAT KIND OF FOOD DOES ERIC LOVE?

☐ FAST FOOD.

☐ DESSERT.

☐ HEALTHY FOOD.

LET'S

LISTEN

1 LISTEN TO THE NAMES OF THE FRUITS.

FRUITS		
APPLE  Andrey Elkin/iStockphoto.com	BANANA  bergamont/Shutterstock.com	GRAPES  ilietus/iStockphoto.com
MANGO  FRANCOIS-EDMOND/ iStockphoto.com	PEAR  atoss/iStockphoto.com	WATERMELON 

2 NOW FIND THE NAMES OF THE FRUITS.

H	P	W	A	T	E	R	M	E	L	O	N
A	E	O	U	O	C	Y	R	Z	G	C	Q
P	B	G	R	A	P	E	S	A	U	H	B
P	X	N	I	A	R	P	G	E	Y	E	A
L	E	Q	M	A	N	G	O	T	K	R	N
E	W	A	J	I	X	G	D	O	T	R	A
V	P	E	A	R	J	B	E	X	R	I	N
F	S	N	V	S	P	I	X	I	W	Z	A

2 COUNT THE NUMBERS.

Claudia Marianno

3 LISTEN AND COLOR.

1 2 3 4 5

6 7 8 9 10

11 12 13 14 15

LET'S PLAY

1 LET'S PLAY WITH NUMBERS.

GraphicsRF/Shutterstock.com

GOOD DEED

EAT FRUIT AND BE HEALTHY!

1 WHAT KIND OF FRUIT DO YOU LIKE?

Oksana Mizina/Shutterstock.com

leonori/iStockphoto.com

2 TRACE THE WORD.

FRUIT

DIGITAL PLAY

CHOOSING YOUR FOOD

- CIRCLE THE HEALTHY FOOD.

Idea Route/Shutterstock.com

Markus Mainka/Shutterstock.com

Idea Route/Shutterstock.com

Markus Mainka/Shutterstock.com

Markus Mainka/Shutterstock.com

Markus Mainka/Shutterstock.com

Markus Mainka/Shutterstock.com

LET'S SING!

DIFFERENT FRUITS IN A TREE

SIX YELLOW BANANAS IN A TREE
ONE LOOKED DOWN AT ME.
I SHOOK THE TREE
AND ONE FELL DOWN... IT WAS AVA!

FOUR GREEN PEARS IN A TREE,
ONE LOOKED DOWN AT ME.
I SHOOK THE TREE
AND ONE FELL DOWN... IT WAS AVA!

SEVEN RED APPLES IN A TREE,
ONE LOOKED DOWN AT ME.
I SHOOK THE TREE
AND ONE FELL DOWN... IT WAS AVA!
[...]

TRADITIONAL NURSERY RHYME: ADAPTED.

Ideario Lab

VOCABULARY

TREE: ÁRVORE.
LOOKED DOWN: OLHOU PARA BAIXO.
SHOOK (TO SHAKE): BALANCEI (BALANÇAR).
FELL DOWN (TO FALL DOWN): CAIU (CAIR).

ENGLISH AROUND THE WORLD

LEARNING ABOUT FRUITS AROUND THE WORLD

THERE ARE SOME TASTY FRUITS AROUND THE WORLD. GET TO KNOW SOME OF THEM.

domnicky/iStockphoto.com

UNITED KINGDOM – ELDERBERRY

akepong srichaichana/Shutterstock.com

AUSTRALIA – FINGER LIME

mr_Prof/iStockphoto.com

NEW ZEALAND – FEIJOA

Candy_Vandy/iStockphoto.com

CANADA – SASKATOON BERRY

- DRAW YOUR FAVORITE FRUIT.

LET'S PLAY

1 COLOR ACCORDING TO THE CAPTION.

- GRAPE / PEAR
- APPLE
- BANANA
- ORANGE

AriffAmin Illustration/Shutterstock.com

2 COUNT.

Gbuglok/Shutterstock.com

Nataliya Schmidt/Shutterstock.com

☐ BANANAS ☐ ORANGES

3 MATCH.

Natykach Nataliia/ Shutterstock.com

AFTER THIS UNIT

I CAN

IDENTIFY FRUITS.			
SAY WHAT MY FAVORITE FRUIT IS.			
USE NUMBERS TO QUANTIFY FRUITS.			
IDENTIFY HEALTHY AND UNHEALTHY FOODS.			

UNIT 7

A VISIT TO THE AQUARIUM

I DON'T KNOW, BUT THAT IS A SHARK.
TODAY IS A SPECIAL DAY!
WOW! WHAT FISH IS THIS?
I'M HAPPY TO BE HERE! THANKS A MILLION, MRS. CARTER.
HOW MANY FISH ARE THERE IN THIS AQUARIUM?

Ideario Lab

VOCABULARY

A SPECIAL DAY: UM DIA ESPECIAL.

THANKS A MILLION!: MUITO OBRIGADO!

WHAT FISH?: QUE PEIXE?

SHARK: TUBARÃO.

HOW MANY: QUANTOS.

ARE THERE: HÁ.

FISH: PEIXE(S).

AQUARIUM: AQUÁRIO.

COMPREHENSION

1 WHERE ARE THE KIDS AND THEIR TEACHER? CHECK.

klyaksun/Shutterstock.com

☐ IN A CIRCUS.

klyaksun/iStockphoto.com

☐ AT THE THEATER.

ONYXprj/iStockphoto.com

☐ IN AN AQUARIUM.

2 WHO IS HAPPY TO BE THERE? CHECK.

☐ JAY. ☐ MIA. ☐ TIM.

LET'S PLAY

1 TRACE THE WORDS.

Microstocker.Pro/Shutterstock.com

SHARK

Anne Koeleman/Shutterstock.com

SEATURTLE

Jemastock/Shutterstock.com

FISH

Soonios Pro/Shutterstock.com

SEAHORSE

LET'S LISTEN

1 LOOK AT THE PICTURES AND LISTEN.

Tomas Kotouc/Shutterstock.com

SHARK.
THE SHARK IS BIG.

ArtEvent ET/iStockphoto.com

FISH.
THE FISH IS SMALL.

vkilikov/Shutterstock.com

SEA TURTLE.
THE SEA TURTLE IS BIG.

Spiridonov Oleg/Shutterstock.com

SEAHORSE.
THE SEAHORSE IS SMALL.

2 ARE THEY BIG OU SMALL? CHECK.

BIG ☐
SMALL ☐

Mykola Sosiukin/iStockphoto.com

Peteri/Shutterstock.com

☐ BIG
☐ SMALL

BIG ☐
SMALL ☐

Liami/Shutterstock.com

AlSimonov/iStockphoto.com

☐ BIG
☐ SMALL

LET'S PLAY

1 TRACE THE RECTANGLES.

A7880S/Shutterstock.com

jsabirova/Shutterstock.com

RECTANGLE.

2 TRACE THE CIRCLES.

Milya Shaykh/Shutterstock.com

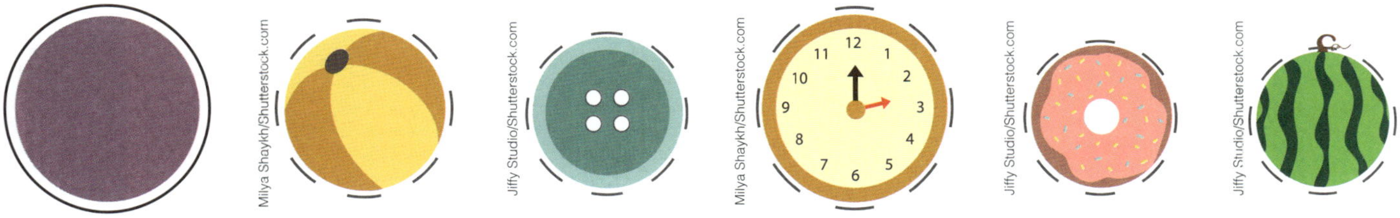

Jiffy Studio/Shutterstock.com Milya Shaykh/Shutterstock.com Jiffy Studio/Shutterstock.com Milya Shaykh/Shutterstock.com Jiffy Studio/Shutterstock.com Jiffy Studio/Shutterstock.com

CIRCLE.

3 MATCH.

Anne Koeleman/Shutterstock.com

SHARK

Microstocker.Pro/Shutterstock.com

SEA TURTLE

Jemastock/Shutterstock.com

SEAHORSE

Soonios Pro/Shutterstock.com

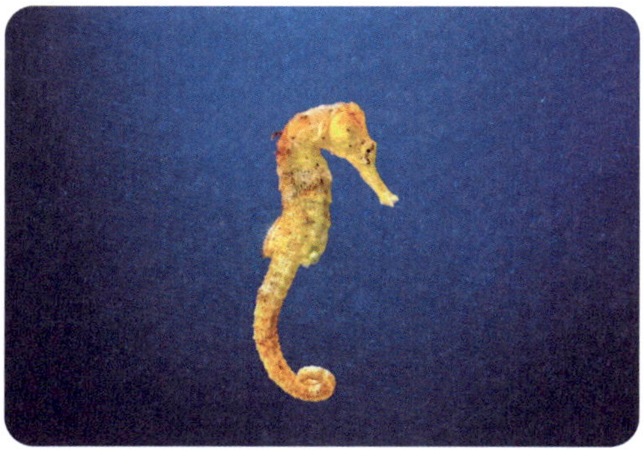

FISH

GOOD DEED

I RESPECT AND CARE FOR MY PLANET

1 BUILD YOUR FISH TANK. PASTE THE STICKERS.

2 TRACE THE WORDS.

SEA TURTLE

FISH

STARFISH

SEAHORSE

LET'S PLAY

1 HOW MANY FISH ARE THERE IN THE FISH TANK?

- [ ] FIVE.
- [ ] SIX.
- [ ] SEVEN.

2 HOW MANY FISH AND TURTLES ARE THERE IN THE FISH TANK?

- [ ] TWO.
- [ ] EIGHT.
- [ ] ELEVEN.

LET'S SING!

A SMALL FISH

A SMALL FISH, A SMALL FISH, A SMALL FISH
HOW MANY FISH CAN YOU SEE?
ONE FISH, FIVE FISH, TEN FISH, AND FIFTEEN.

THEY PLAY AND SWIM, PLAY AND SWIM, PLAY AND SWIM.
AND HOW ARE YOU? HOW ARE YOU? HOW ARE YOU?
I'M SO HAPPY, SO HAPPY, SO HAPPY.
DOO DOO DOO DOO DOO DOO (CHORUS)

THE SONG WAS ADAPTED FOR THIS BOOK.

Ideario Lab

VOCABULARY

SMALL: PEQUENO.
FISH: PEIXE(S).
HOW MANY?: QUANTOS?
CAN YOU SEE?: VOCÊ PODE VER?
PLAY: BRINCAM (BRINCAR).
SWIM: NADAM (NADAR).
HOW ARE YOU?: COMO VOCÊ ESTÁ?
HAPPY: FELIZ.

ENGLISH AROUND THE WORLD

GETTING TO KNOW AN AQUARIUM

- DO YOU LIKE SEA ANIMALS?

BLUE HORIZON AQUARIUM OF CANADA

CREATE A SENSATION

IN THE HEART OF CANADA.

EDUCATIONAL PROGRAMS BECAUSE NATURE IS IMPORTANT

- For all ages
- Student career exploration
- Interactive virtual tours

COME VISIT THE AQUARIUM!

DIGITAL PLAY

1 FIND AND CIRCLE THE SEA ANIMALS.

exxorian/iStockphoto.com

2 TRACE THE WORDS.

AQUARIUM

SEA ANIMALS

LET'S PLAY

1 TRACE AND COLOR.

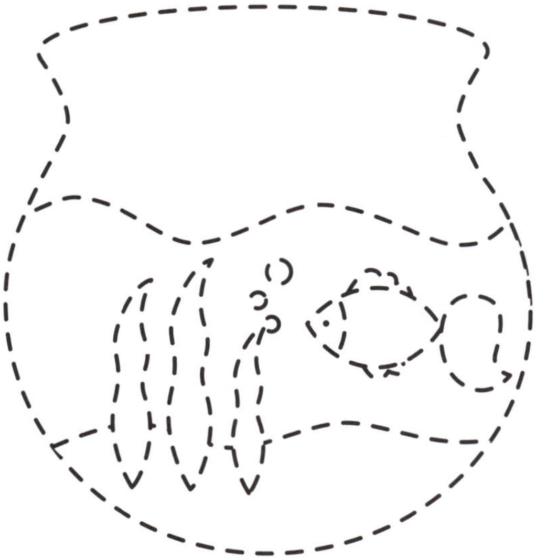

Milya Shaykh/Shutterstock.com

AFTER THIS UNIT I CAN

IDENTIFY SEA ANIMALS.			
DESCRIBE SEA ANIMALS.			
RECOGNIZE GEOMETRIC SHAPES.			
TALK ABOUT CARING FOR THE PLANET.			

UNIT 8

TRASH? OH NO!

LET'S THROW THE TRASH IN THE RECYCLING BINS. WHAT DO YOU HAVE?
I HAVE PLASTIC SPOONS.
I HAVE A SODA CAN.
ORGANIC
PLASTIC
PAPER
METAL
GLASS
GREAT, KIDS! LET'S SORT OUR WASTE AND TAKE CARE OF THE ENVIRONMENT.
I HAVE A GLASS BOTTLE.
I HAVE A BANANA PEEL.
I HAVE A PAPER PLATE.
Ideario Lab

VOCABULARY

LET'S THROW: VAMOS JOGAR.

RECYCLING: RECICLAGEM.

BINS: LIXEIRAS.

SPOONS: COLHERES.

SODA CAN: LATA DE REFRIGERANTE.

BOTTLE: GARRAFA.

BANANA PEEL: CASCA DE BANANA.

PAPER PLATE: PRATO DE PAPEL.

SORT OUR WASTE: SEPARAR NOSSO LIXO.

ENVIRONMENT: AMBIENTE.

COMPREHENSION

1 MATCH THE KIDS' OBJECTS WITH THE CORRESPONDING MATERIAL.

Ideario Lab

Vector Tradition/Shutterstock.com

EgudinKa/Shutterstock.com

gerenme/iStockphoto.com

LET'S

LISTEN

1 LISTEN AND PASTE THE RECYCLING BINS.

LET'S PLAY

1 HELP JAY SORT OUT THE WASTE.

StockSmartStart/Shutterstock.com

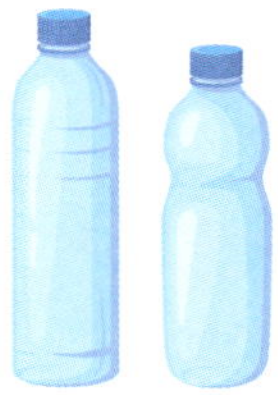

lotos_land/Shutterstock.com

VELvector/Shutterstock.com

lemono/Shutterstock.com

Tran Thi Thuy Ha/Shutterstock.com

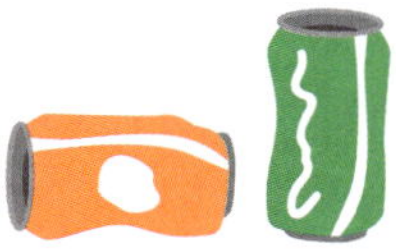

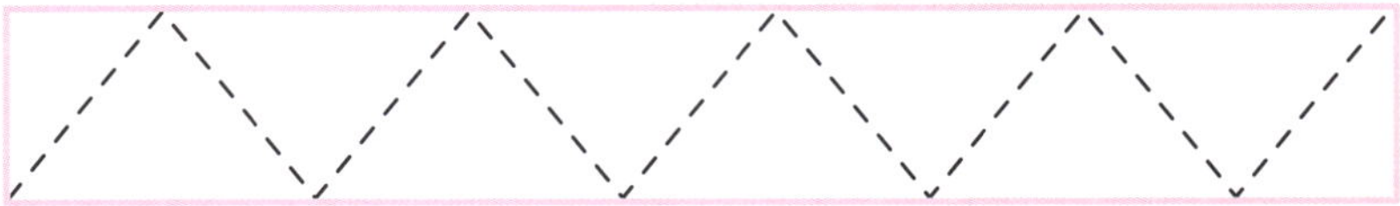

Spyro the Dragon/Shutterstock.com

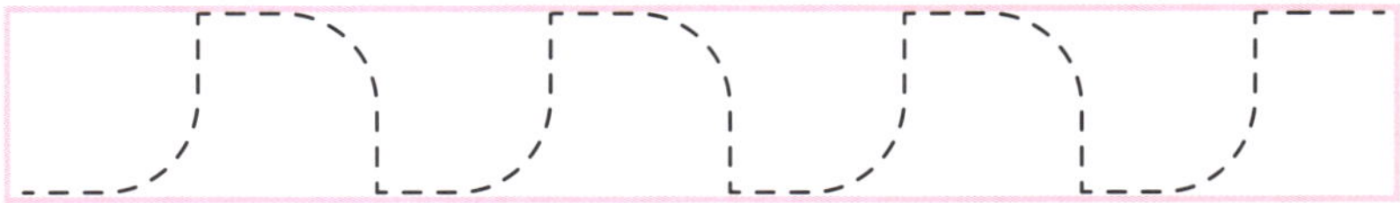

LET'S SING!

RECYCLING HELPS THE EARTH!

PAPER IN THE BLUE CAN, THAT'S THE WAY TO START.
RECYCLING HELPS THE EARTH, IT'S SO SMART!
METAL IN THE YELLOW CAN... IT'S EASY, YOU'LL SEE,
LET'S SAVE OUR PLANET FOR YOU AND ME!

GLASS GOES IN THE CAN THAT'S SO BRIGHT,
WE'RE DOING WHAT'S RIGHT, WE FEEL THE LIGHT,
PLASTIC IN THE RED CAN, THAT'S WHERE IT BELONGS,
WITH EACH LITTLE ACTION, WE'RE SINGING THE EARTH SONG.

AND NOW, MY LITTLE FRIEND, DON'T FORGET THIS PART,
THE BROWN CAN IS FOR FOOD, IT'S A BRAND-NEW START,
COMPOSTING HELPS THE EARTH, IT'S THE FINAL PIECE,
TAKING CARE OF OUR WORLD BRINGS US PEACE!

CREATED SPECIALLY FOR THE BOOK.

VOCABULARY

THE WAY TO START: A MANEIRA DE COMEÇAR.
RECYCLING: RECICLAGEM.
BRIGHT: BRILHANTE.
LITTLE ACTION: PEQUENA AÇÃO.
TAKING CARE: CUIDAR.
WORLD: MUNDO.
PEACE: PAZ.

LET'S PLAY

1 CIRCLE THE CORRESPONDING PICTURE.

PLASTIC

Natykach Nataliia/Shutterstock.com

StockSmartStart/Shutterstock.com

klyaksun/Shutterstock.com

METAL

Natykach Nataliia/Shutterstock.com

vinap/Shutterstock.com

klyaksun/Shutterstock.com

GLASS

ann_ounce/Shutterstock.com

vi73/Shutterstock.com

Natykach Nataliia/Shutterstock.com

PAPER

mollicart/Shutterstock.com

Mr.Timoty/Shutterstock.com

karandaev/iStockphotos.com

ENGLISH AROUND THE WORLD

EARTH DAY

THE ACTIONS THAT HELP THE PLANET ARE REDUCING, REUSING, AND RECYCLING.

wongmbatuloyo/iStockphoto.com

DIGITAL PLAY

REDUCE, REUSE, AND RECYCLE

- LET'S REDUCE, REUSE, AND RECYCLE WASTE TO PROTECT THE ENVIRONMENT.

Rawpixel.com/Shutterstock.com

LET'S PLAY

1 TRACE THE WORDS.

StockSmartStart/Shutterstock.com

PLASTIC

PLASTIC

Flas100/Shutterstock.com

PAPER

PAPER

mollicart/Shutterstock.com

GLASS

GLASS

Rolling Stones/Shutterstock.com

METAL

METAL

Magicleaf/Shutterstock.com

ORGANIC

ORGANIC

2 LOOK AT THE PICTURE AND COUNT THE ITEMS.

Idearío Lab

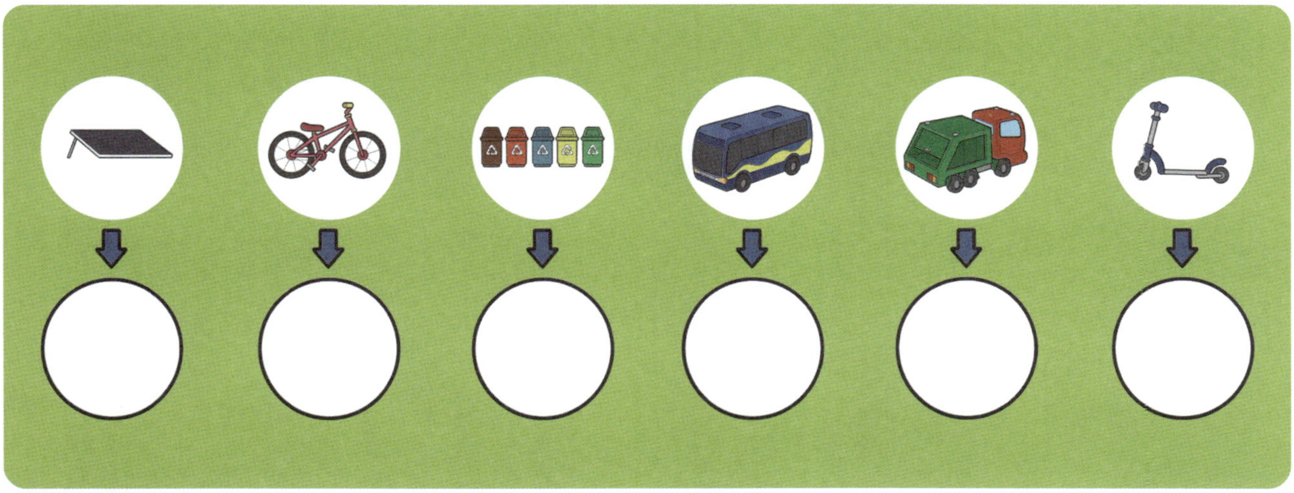

GOOD DEED

A FAIR-TRADE SCHOOL CAMPAIGN

1 LET'S EXCHANGE USED TOYS AND OTHER OBJECTS! PASTE THE STICKERS.

Ideario Lab

AFTER THIS UNIT

I CAN

IDENTIFY DIFFERENT TYPES OF TRASH.			
UNDERSTAND HOW TO SEPARATE TRASH.			
REFLECT ON THE IMPORTANCE OF REDUCING, REUSING, AND RECYCLING.			
RECOGNIZE THE DIFFERENT COLORS OF TRASH BINS.			

REVIEW

UNIT 1

1 TRACE THE WORD.

Ideario Lab

HELLO

HELLO

2 COLOR.

Castleski/Shutterstock.com

HAPPY.

Great Vector Elements/Shutterstock.com

CREATIVE.

Castleski/Shutterstock.com

ANGRY.

UNIT 2

1 TRACE THE LINES.

KoAlia_draws/Shutterstock.com
JUMP

KoAlia_draws/Shutterstock.com

KoAlia_draws/ Shutterstock.com
PLAY

KoAlia_draws/Shutterstock.com

AlonzoDesign/iStockphoto.com
RUN

Yana Lesnik/Shutterstock.com

2 CONNECT THE DOTS AND COLOR.

natchapohn/Shutterstock.com

I CAN RIDE A BIKE.

UNIT 3

1 TRACE THE NUMBERS AND COUNT.

jehsomwang/Shutterstock.com

UNIT 4

1 TAKE THE SPIDER-MAN TO THE CITY.

LesiaArt/Shutterstock.com

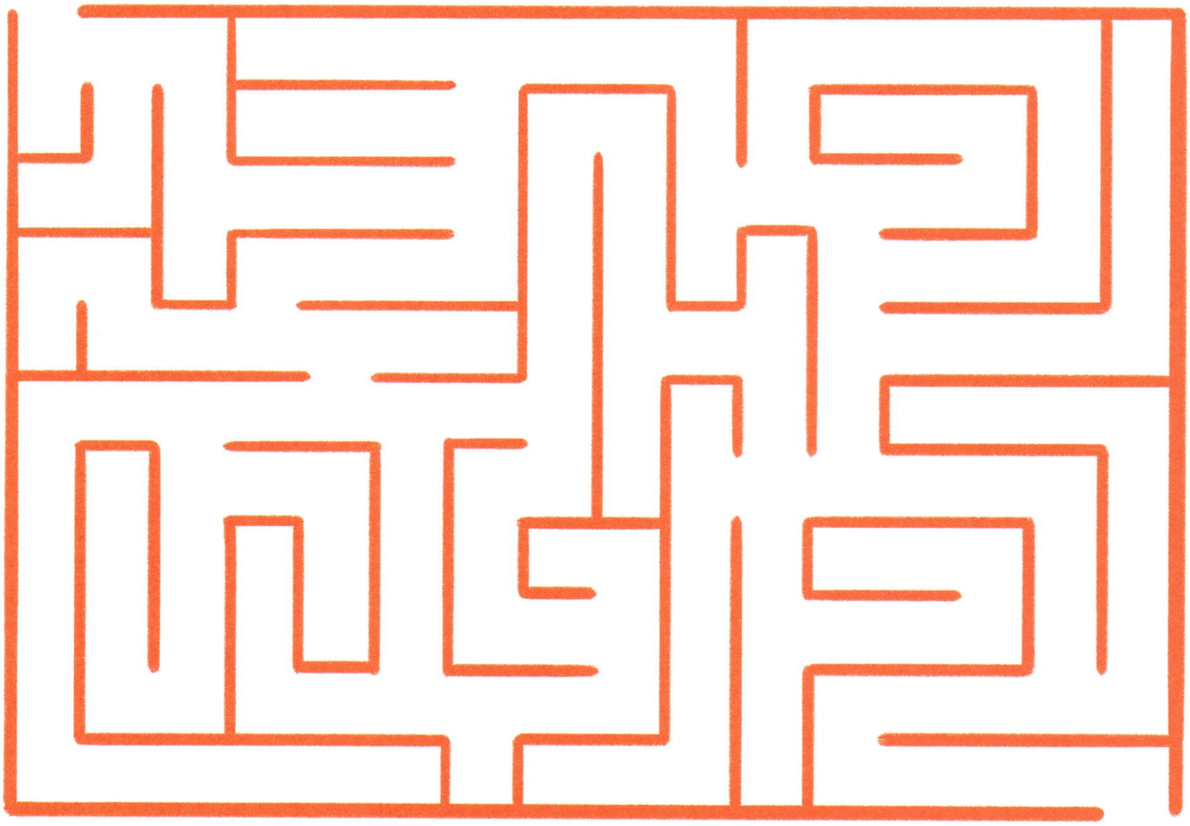

Claudia Marianno

ZiroGraphix/Shutterstock.com

UNIT 5

1 WHICH PICTURES SHOW POSITIVE ATTITUDES? CHECK.

Wat cartoon/Shutterstock.com

Tenstudio/Shutterstock.com

gbmotiongfx/Shutterstock.com

yusufdemirci/Shutterstock.com

UNIT 6

1 MATCH.

Colorfuel Studio/Shutterstock.com

HappyPictures/Shutterstock.com

Gurzzza/iStockphoto.com

CoolFinger/Shutterstock.com

KanKhem/iStockphoto.com

Armation/Shutterstock.com

UNIT 7

1 TRACE THE WORD.

Godruma/iStockphoto.com

FISH

FISH

pornpimoln Puangsai/iStockphoto.com

SEA TURTLE

SEA TURTLE

A Mokhtari/iStockphoto.com

SEAHORSE

SEAHORSE

Microstocker.Pro/Shutterstock.com

SHARK

SHARK

REVIEW

UNIT 8

1 MATCH.

lotos_land/Shutterstock.com

Tranle/Shutterstock.com

Victoria Sergeeva/Shutterstock.com

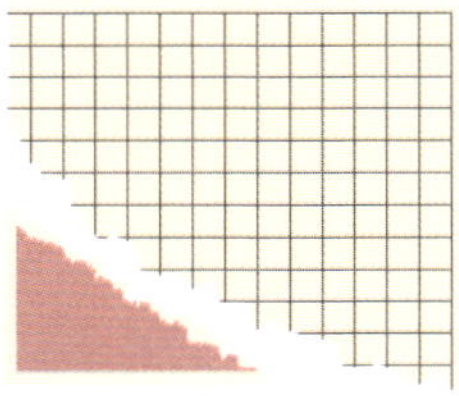

Alina Kolyuka/Shutterstock.com

vertolena/Shutterstock.com

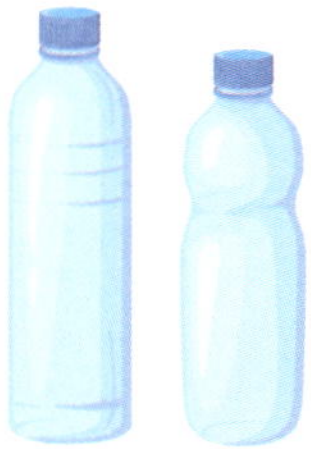

StockSmartStart/Shutterstock.com

PICTURE DICTIONARY

A

Monory/Shutterstock.com

AIRPLANE

JosepPerianes/Shutterstock.com

ANGRY

ONYXprj/iStockphoto.com

AQUARIUM

Spreadthesign/Shutterstock.com

ARM

B

klyaksun/Shutterstock.com

BATHROOM

Sofia Kalach/iStockphoto.com

BEACH

klyaksun/Shutterstock.com

BEDROOM

Mintoboru/Shutterstock.com

BIKE

djmilic/Shutterstock.com

BIN

Colorfuel Studio/Shutterstock.com

BRAVE

DEHIL MAKSYM/Shutterstock.com

BRIGHT

Shutterstock.com/robuart

BUS

C

Igogosha/Shutterstock.com

CAR

Janis Abolins/Shutterstock.com

CARROT

ghenadie/Shutterstock.com

CAT

klyaksun/Shutterstock.com

CIRCUS

Norbert9/Shutterstock.com

CITY

Shawn Hempel/Shutterstock.com

CIRCLE

Golden Sikorka/Shutterstock.com

CONDOMINIUM

Lana Way/Shutterstock.com

COUNTRYSIDE

D

PeN2light/Shutterstock.com

DAUGHTER

yavi/Shutterstock.com

DODGEBALL

Tartila/Shutterstock.com

DOLPHIN

E

Jane Kelly/Shutterstock.com

EARTH

Spreadthesign/Shutterstock.com

ELEPHANT

Setia Abadi Art/Shutterstock.com

EMOJIS

F

Jemastock/Shutterstock.com

FISH

charnsitr/Shutterstock.com

FLAG

robuart/Shutterstock.com

FOOD

ActiveLines/Shutterstock.com

FOREST

G

Iconic Bestiary/Shutterstock.com

GAMING

Sketch Master/Shutterstock.com

GIRAFFE

StockSmartStart/Shutterstock.com

GLASS WASTE

Igillustrator/Shutterstock.com

GOOD

Gurza/Shutterstock.com

GRAPE

Seahorse Vector/ Shutterstock.com

GYMNASIUM

H

Eugene B-sov/ Shutterstock.com

HAPPY

Magyro/Shutterstock.com

HAT

grmarc/Shutterstock.com

HEART

FoxyImage/Shutterstock.com

HEROES

exxorian/iStockphoto.com

HIDE-AND-SEEK

Veyselcelikdemir/Shutterstock.com

HOPSCOTCH

J

Valeriia Soloveva/ Shutterstock

JELLY

Tenstudio/Shutterstock

JUMP

L

Roman Kybus/Shutterstock

LADYBUG

klyaksun/Shutterstock

LAUNDRY ROOM

mickallnice/Shutterstock

LOSER

M

inspiring.team/Shutterstock.com

MALL

FARBAI/Shutterstock

MANGO

yogasitamas/Shutterstock

METAL WASTE

Mastak A/Shutterstock

MOUSE

klyaksun/Shutterstock

MUSEUM

N

Vector Cool Arts/Shutterstock

NEWT

O

sundatoon/Shutterstock

OCTOPUS

StockSmartStart/Shutterstock

ORGANIC WASTE

P

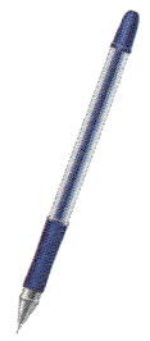
Duda Vasilii/Shutterstock.com

PEN

Microstocker.Pro/ Shutterstock.com

PICNIC

NishanDesigns/Shutterstock

PIG

Yindee/Shutterstock.com

POLICE OFFICER

TanyaBegun/Shutterstock.com

PRINCESS

R

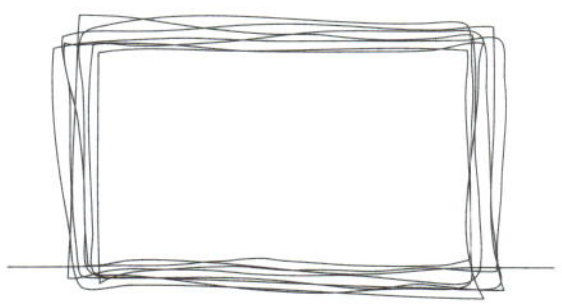
Kamila Bay/Shutterstock

RECTANGLE

Gvardgraph/Shutterstock.com

RESTAURANT

Colorfuel Studio/Shutterstock

RUN

S

Perfect_kebab/Shutterstock

SAND

vectortatu/Shutterstock

SEA

Sudowoodo/Shutterstock

SEAHORSE

Kastoluza/Shutterstock

SHARK

Johnny Dream/Shutterstock

STARFISH

CoolFinger/Shutterstock

STUDENTS

T

IconicBestiary/iStockphoto.com

TAG

Colorfuel Studio/Shutterstock

TEAM

the8monkey/Shutterstock.com

THEATER

V

Qualit Design/Shutterstock

VACATION

W

ChekmanDaria/Shutterstock

WI-FI

INDEX OF SONGS

UNIT 1
HELLO, HELLO, HELLO 27

UNIT 2
I CAN DO MANY THINGS! 37

UNIT 3
I LIKE VIDEO GAMES 51

UNIT 4
DO YOU WANT TO BE A HERO? 62

UNIT 5
FAMILY VACATIONS 74

UNIT 6
DIFFERENT FRUITS IN A TREE 85

UNIT 7
A SMALL FISH 97

UNIT 8
RECYCLING HELPS THE EARTH! 105

INDEX OF LISTENINGS

UNIT 1

SCHOOL FRIENDS 19
THE ALPHABET 22
LISTEN AND COLOR 25

UNIT 2

FUN TIME 31
BODY PARTS 33

UNIT 3

ONLINE GAMES 43
GAMING TERMS 45
LISTEN TO THE NUMBERS 48

UNIT 4

MY HEROES 53
I AM A HERO / A HEROIN 56
LISTEN TO THE WORDS 59

UNIT 5

FAMILY VACATION 67
MEANS OF TRANSPORTATION 70
COLORS 73

UNIT 6

HEALTHY FOOD 79
FRUITS 81
NUMBERS 82

UNIT 7

A VISIT TO THE AQUARIUM 89
SEA ANIMALS 92

UNIT 8

TRASH? OH NO! 101
LISTEN AND PASTE THE RECYCLING BINS 103

VALENTINE'S DAY

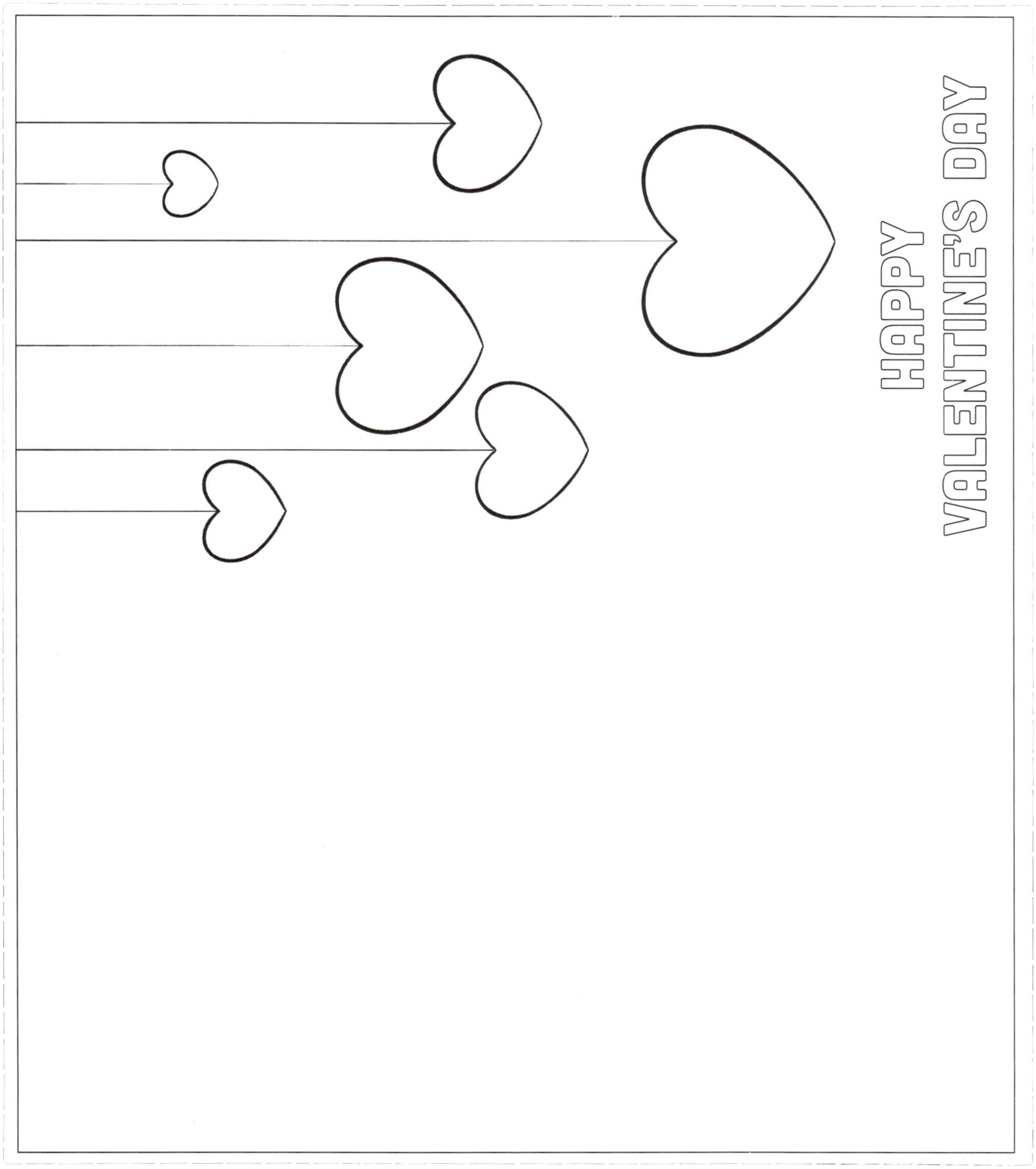
HAPPY
VALENTINE'S DAY

Ideario Lab

EASTER

MOTHER'S DAY

FRENTE VERSO

FATHER'S DAY

32 pixels/Shutterstock.com

CHILDREN'S DAY

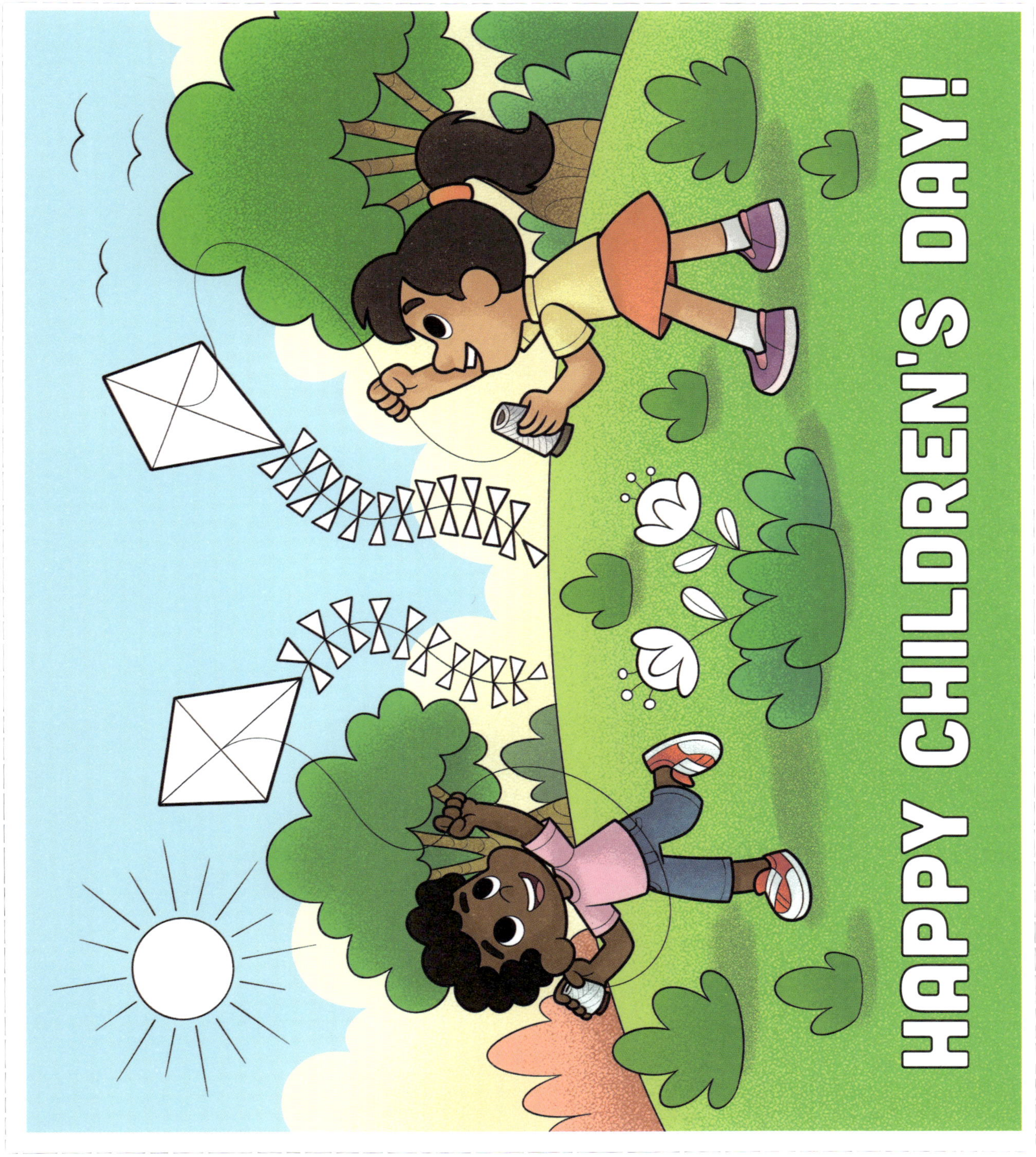
HAPPY CHILDREN'S DAY!

Ideario Lab

TEACHER'S DAY

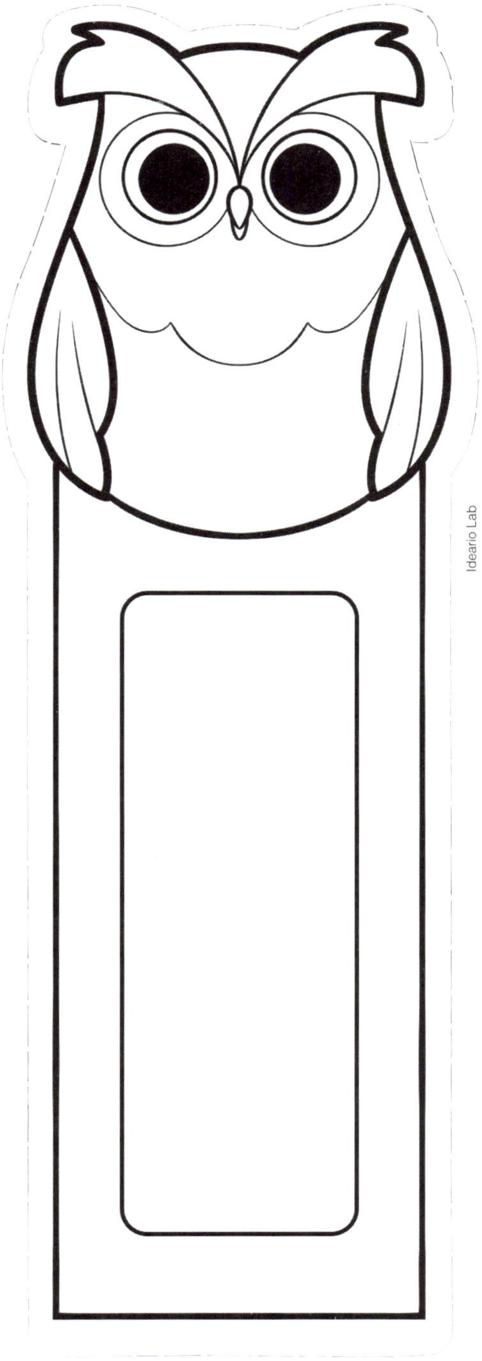

THANKSGIVING DAY

CHRISTMAS

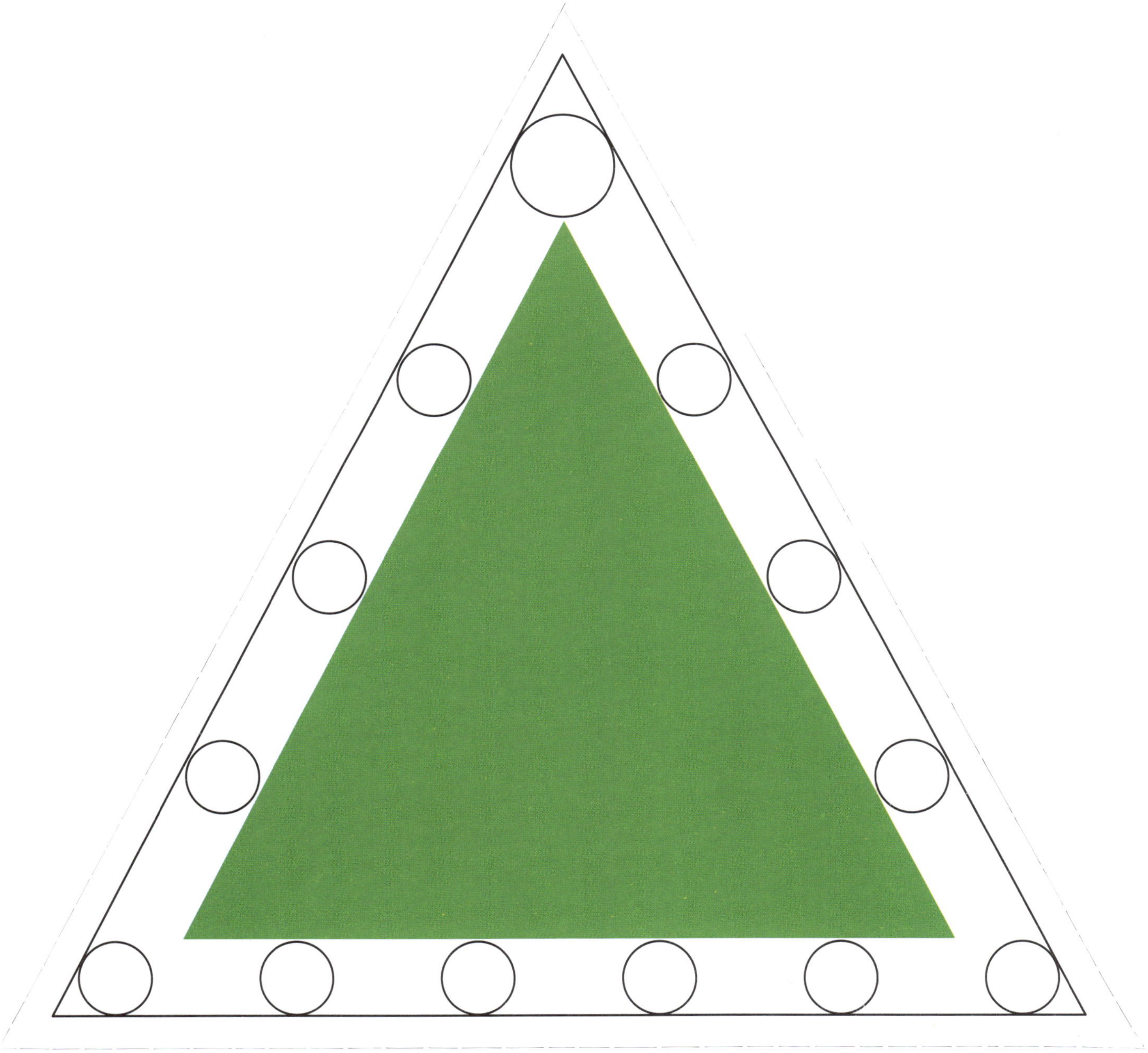

Acervo editora

PAGE 11

Ideario Lab

PAGE 26

Tranle/Shutterstock.com

Emil Timplaru/Shutterstock.com

Edge Creative/Shutterstock.com

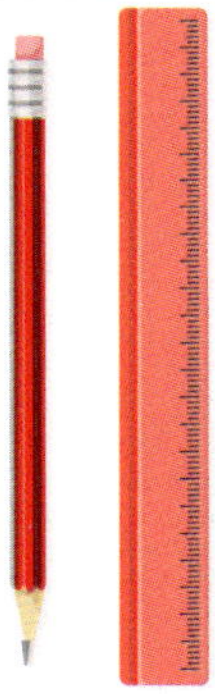

onebluelight/iStockphoto.com

Olena Dumanchuk/iStockphoto.com

PAGE 30

Castleski/Shutterstock.com

Castleski/Shutterstock.com

Great Vector Elements/Shutterstock.com

PAGE 33

PAGE 46

kiyaksun/Shutterstock.com

graphic-line/Shutterstock.com

GraphicsRF/Shutterstock.com

ALEK7/SHUTTERSTOCK.COM

robuart/Shutterstock.com

PAGE 66

Aratehortua/Shutterstock.com

adekvat/iStockphoto.com

Aratehortua/Shutterstock.com

Virinaflora/Shutterstock.com

PAGE 72

Ideario Lab

PAGE 95

ONYXprj/ iStockphoto.com

tatianazaets/ iStockphoto.com

clairevis/iStockphoto.com

AhNinniah/ iStockphoto.com

ONYXprj/iStockphoto.com

PAGE 103

lotos_land/Shutterstock.com

PAGE 110

Ideario Lab